Anonymous

The Connecticut real estate register

Anonymous

The Connecticut real estate register

ISBN/EAN: 9783337733230

Printed in Europe, USA, Canada, Australia, Japan

Cover: Foto ©ninafisch / pixelio.de

More available books at **www.hansebooks.com**

THE

CONNECTICUT

REAL ESTATE REGISTER:

(PUBLISHED SEMI-ANNUALLY.)

COPY-RIGHT SECURED.

PUBLISHED FOR GRATUITOUS CIRCULATION

BY

Cornelius A. Lincoln,

REAL ESTATE AGENT,

Connecticut Real Estate Office, No. 265 Main Street,

HARTFORD, CONN.

HARTFORD:
PRESS OF CASE, LOCKWOOD AND COMPANY.
1868.

INTRODUCTION.

In presenting the public with the first number of the Connecticut Real Estate Register, a few words of explanation may seem necessary. It certainly will be no news to the intelligent business people of our State to say that there has always existed a great necessity for a first-class Connecticut Real Estate Register; a work that should become particularly identified with the interests of real estate owners, and purchasers, in our State,—and a work to be recognized as authority upon all matters pertaining to the real estate business. Without further preface, we will say, that, in the Connecticut Real Estate Register which we have established, we shall endeavor to furnish such a work, and shall also try, to the very best of our ability, to maintain the good standing of our profession.

We have determined to make The Connecticut Real Estate Register *a permanent institution*, although the expense attending the publication and circulation of it will be very large. It is our intention to issue it semi-annually; and its pages will contain a *reliable descriptive list* of the largest number of desirable FARMS, COUNTRY RESIDENCES, VILLAGE AND CITY PROPERTY, MILLS AND MANUFACTORIES, HOTELS, STORES, BUILDING LOTS, LIVERY STABLES, BUSINESS CHANCES, &c., &c., to be found registered for sale at *any real estate agency in New England*. It will also contain leading and important articles of interest to the buyer and seller as regards the state of the markets as affecting real estate, &c.

To every FARMER or owner of real estate, who may advertise their property for sale in its columns, — and to the PURCHASER, — it will prove an *invaluable work*, and supply the want long felt by thousands of buyers and sellers who are daily seeking new homes in our State; and a work greatly needed by myself in my own extensive business for a period of ten years, as a medium of *public communication between buyer and seller to be reached in no other way*, and to aid me in sustaining in the future, as in the past, our unrivalled preeminence as the *first among real estate brokers*. If you have a FARM or REAL

ESTATE of *any description* to dispose of, you will find this the *very best* and by far the *cheapest* mode of making known among *actual buyers* just what you have for sale; as I send to the very man who *wants to buy* a full and accurate description of your property in each copy of the REGISTER.

It will be CIRCULATED GRATUITOUSLY, in order that people in every section of the country may let their friends and neighbors who are seeking new homes, know of the *large* and varied list of desirable real estate offered for sale at the *old established* CONNECTICUT REAL ESTATE OFFICE, and to induce them to seek our beautiful homes, our healthy climate, and prolific soil; our valuable water powers, mills, and manufactories, schools, &c.,—instead of incurring the *fearful risk* of locating themselves and families in the *fever-ridden* sections of other States. I propose to advertise everything in a full and explicit manner, and to *faithfully* and *impartially* represent, as heretofore, whatever I may offer for sale; and shall use care to always *avoid exaggeration*, that all may rely upon the description given as *correct and truthful*, so that the purchaser will find the property *as it is represented to be;* and need make but one journey to find just the property he wants.

There are thousands daily seeking *Farms, Country Residences, Business Chances, &c. &c.*, in our State for purchase. They all need some *reliable* and *central* authority, where they can obtain a complete and accurate list of the greater portion of the property for sale in our State. Now they are obliged to purchase papers day after day, and then seldom find what they want. The CONNECTICUT REAL ESTATE REGISTER will be a work which they can lay their hands upon at any time, "*free*," and find in its columns the greater portion of the desirable property for sale in this State, and best adapted to their wants.

Since we have announced our intention to publish the Register, we have received from ten to twenty letters daily, from parties wishing to purchase property of every description, — wishing the Register sent to them, &c. We now have over 3,000 names of those wishing the REGISTER, and shall obtain the balance of our subscribers by advertising it in the daily and weekly papers, "sent free to any address," besides distributing from *thirty to fifty per day among actual buyers who call at our office.* We shall also distribute them in all the principal hotels, eating-houses, steamboats, railway stations, &c. &c.; in a word, *we intend to keep* THE CONNECTICUT REAL ESTATE REGISTER *before the people.*

Those wishing to buy in any particular locality, will be furnished with full descriptions of all we have, and as we are receiving new property for sale every day, and have much valuable property NOT *advertised in the* REGISTER *or* PAPERS, parties not finding what they want should communicate with us before purchasing. *No trouble to comply with your wishes, and no charge to buyers whatever.* We ask you to consult your own interest, by paying us a visit, or write to us, and we will gladly furnish you with all the information in our power.

In sending for a more definite description of any property, please give the *number* at the top, also the town in which it is located. It was our intention to have the Register contain a description of about 500 farms that we have for sale; but after reflection, we thought best to place in it only those that had been left for sale recently, thereby presenting to those wishing to purchase a *fresh collection* that have not been long in the market. *This issue will not contain those received since Oct. 15th;* and as we shall receive *hundreds before April 1st, next,* parties about to purchase should examine our list at the office.

As we have, for years, sold more real estate than all other brokers in Connecticut combined, and are now doing a larger business than ever before, it is hardly necessary for us to say to *those wishing to buy, sell or exchange* property of any description, that they will find it *greatly to their advantage* to deal at the old established Connecticut Real Estate Office. OUR MOTTO IS THIS: *No sale, no pay; and no charge to the purchaser under any circumstances.* We charge, for selling real estate outside of Hartford, two and one-half per cent. on the price obtained, *the same as we have charged heretofore, notwithstanding the largely increased expense of advertising in the papers, and of issuing* THE CONNECTICUT REAL ESTATE REGISTER. AUCTION SALES, and *special sales,* will be charged special rates, to be ascertained on application.

The FEE FOR ADVERTISING IN THE REGISTER we have fixed at $10; and this amount *will be deducted from the commission when the property is sold.* Those who have *previously* paid us for advertising in the papers, can have theirs inserted in the REGISTER, on receipt of five dollars, which will also *apply on commission.* This, in reality, is but advancing a small portion of the commission to have your property disposed of; and when a party is willing to advance that small portion of the fees, then we are satisfied he really wants to sell; and we are ready to go ahead and use our *best efforts* to dispose of his property, and *pay out our own money also in advertising it liberally in the papers.* We take it for granted when we receive the small fee required, you are desirous of selling out.

In sending us a description of your property, be careful to fill out a *correct* and full description.

Those having property for sale, will find the Register the medium through which they can dispose of it *quickly, and at less expense than in any other way.*

Blanks will be furnished (free), on application, to parties who desire to avail themselves of our services; and they should send a minute and correct description, with lowest price, terms, &c.; and *if desiring to advertise,* enclose the Register fee of ten dollars, which will apply on commission, and your property will be *liberally advertised* in the Register and in the NEWSPAPERS; also a description will be placed on file in our office, which is thronged continually.

N. B. No description will be placed in the next number of the Register unless the fee is sent in, with the description.

OFFICE OPEN DAY AND EVENING, and myself, or competent assistants, are always in attendance to give the desired information.

Very truly yours,

C. A. LINCOLN.

THE REAL ESTATE MARKET.

WITH the more favorable weather we have had of late, the demand for every variety of real estate is *greater with us than at any period during the past eleven years.* Houses and tenements for rent, are scarce. We need a great increase in the numbers of good comfortable houses, of moderate size and rent. Our MECHANICS, and others, and the stranger who would locate with us,—if they were to be had,—want them : *Hartford capitalists should protect and shelter her mechanics,* for *they* have made *them,* and *our city,* WEALTHY IN MANUFACTURES, and if encouraged to remain with us, by giving them comfortable homes, at moderate cost, they will build up for Hartford a still greater fame. But houses of this class in the city are not readily found, and many are *obliged* to seek property for purchase; and as property in the city is high, very many are purchasing in the country. Cheap residence, and farm property, is in great demand with us, as this class of people are prepared to BUY A CHEAP PROPERTY, (*and pay interest if need be,*) rather than hire at present rates ; and so soon as we offer anything desirable, in city or country, at prices ranging from $1,500, to $6,000, it is taken at once. There is considerable speculative inquiries for residence and business property, and large estates, which can be divided up, and sold out again in parcels. We dispose of an immense amount of *city, and farm property especially,* and could sell much more if good desirable places could be had. Property in many parts of our city and State *cannot fail to prove a profitable investment,* as it is *rapidly enhancing* in value; and at present prices, although some are offered largely in advance of former rates, are still *very reasonable,* considering *the certainty of the rapid increase in value.* We offer a large amount of property at former prices, much of which is for sale in consequence of old age, infirmity, business changes, &c., *rendering a disposal absolutely necessary :* consequently, *bargains are offered.* We can give no better advice to any one than to *secure a bargain when you can ;* and *we know* that such *we are constantly offering,* and *this issue* of the REGISTER *contains very many of them.*

All classes of real estate, *in desirable locations,* are *sure to go up higher* ; and any property bought *now,* will bring a good profit in a short time. *We feel sure of this,* and our advice is, *not to delay* when you *can* secure *a good bargain. Now* is the time to *buy ;* and a careful examination of THE CONNECTICUT REAL ESTATE REGISTER will show you where good investments may be had.

REAL ESTATE REGISTER.

200 acres,	No. 4001,	$37.50 per acre.

In FARMINGTON, near the center of the town, and only eleven miles from Hartford; the land is under high cultivation, well watered, fenced, &c.; forty acres of young wood-land, fourteen years' growth; great abundance of choice fruit; location very pleasant; bounded south on Farmington river; has a nice two story and L house, wood and hog house, front picket fence, &c., all painted white; horse barn, carriage house, granary, barn, &c. : stock and tools for sale if wanted; terms easy.

70 acres,	No. 4002,	$6,500

In BLOOMFIELD, 2½ miles from Tariffville; farm is in a good state of cultivation, suitably divided into mowing, tillage, and pasturage: land lies towards the sun, is smooth and level, uses machine, &c.; the buildings are in good repair, and consist of a two story house, with wood house painted and blinded, one large barn, and nice new tobacco barn, size 24 x 76, with basement; fruit orchard of six acres; five acres woodland.

130 acres,	No. 4006,	$10,000

In MANCHESTER, seven miles from Hartford; choice land, excellent buildings; pleasantly situated; one of the best farms in town.

50 acres,	No. 4008,	$3,000

In SCOTLAND, WINDHAM COUNTY; buildings and five acres are located in the Center, fronting the village green; abundance of select fruit in great varieties; nice two story house, in fine order, modern style, French plate window-glass in front, &c.; good barn and sheds; water in the house; the balance of the land is located just out of the village, from one-half to one mile, well watered and newly fenced; will sell the five acres and buildings for $2,000, or the whole as above.

163 acres,	No. 4009,	$3,300

In MARLBORO,' on a turnpike road, within one-fourth mile of school, &c.; fifty-five acres of wood-land; the balance is suitably divided, and well watered;

a variety of select fruit; has a good two story house with L, and wood house painted white and blinded, two barns, wagon house, &c.; the above offers a rare chance for a profitable investment.

2 acres,	No. 4016,	$800

In North Windham Village, near church, school, post office, store, cotton, woolen, and thread mills, carriage shops, &c.; nearly new $1\frac{1}{2}$ story house, with front picket fence, both painted white, barn, wood house, and shop; forty fruit trees, vines, &c.

250 acres,	No. 4010,	$4,500

In Moodus, divided into three separate parcels; the house, two barns, &c., with 100 acres of land, well divided into mowing, tillage, and woodland; is located within one mile of the village, and in full view. One parcel of more than 100 acres, with a fine growth of wood, with barn, &c., within one half mile of the above; the balance, located on the same road, one-half mile beyond; stock, crops, and tools for sale.

135 acres,	No. 4011,	$4,500

In Southington, $4\frac{1}{2}$ miles from the city of Meriden; well located, near large paper mills; thirty-five acres woodland; has a splendid fish pond; aqueduct water in the yard; good house, two barns with basements, wagon house, granary, &c.; will sell buildings, with less land, if wanted.

275 acres,	No. 4013,	$5,500

In West Granville, Mass., a splendid stock farm, located twenty miles west of Springfield; will keep thirty head of stock; can easily be made to cut over 100 tons of hay; fine orchards, usually producing from 400 to 600 barrels of choice fruit; sugar-maple orchard; quantity of oak and chestnut timber; farm is well fenced, and is considered the best in town; buildings are good, and cannot be built for the price of the farm; two story house of thirteen rooms, three barns, two good wells, and pure spring water in two yards by aqueduct; stock and tools for sale.

6 acres,	No. 4014,	$6,500

In East Hartford, on Main St., near church, rail road station, post office, &c.; land A No. 1 for gardening; fifty select fruit trees in full bearing; grapes, small fruits, &c.; has a spacious mansion house, a tenement house, a tobacco house, sufficient for $2\frac{1}{2}$ acres of large growth tobacco, with barns and outbuildings: as a village residence, a good and profitable investment, and being located so contiguous to Hartford, and of easy and frequent access render it very inviting and desirable.

200,	No. 4017,	$6,000

In East Glastenbury, ten miles from Hartford; fifty acres of timber land; one-half of it very heavy growth, balance well divided, fenced, and watered; fifteen acres of orcharding; good one story and L house, new grater cider mill, two barns, one new with basement; can keep over thirty head of stock; seven good wells on the farm; aqueduct water to the buildings, but not in order at the present time; well located, one-half mile of school: terms one-half cash.

154 acres,	No. 4018,	$2,700

In UNION, two miles from the Center; twenty-five acres of valuable wood and timber; balance suitably divided, under good cultivation, and well watered; large two story house with L, barn, carriage house, woodhouse, sheds, and hog house; will sell 123 acres and buildings for $2,200.

110 acres,	No. 4020,	$1,500

In EASTFORD, on a turnpike road; near school and churches; *wood and timber enough on the farm to pay for it;* a good variety of fruit; good 1½ story house with L, two barns, one nearly new, wood house, &c.; offered very low, terms easy.

75 acres,	No. 4022,	$2,000

In NEW HARTFORD, one-half mile from school, 1¼ miles from Baker-ville and New Hartford Center; ten acres of fine timber land; sixty-five acres well divided, fenced and watered; abundance of orcharding; 1½ story house, two barns, one nearly new.

40 acres,	No. 4023,	$1,000

In WINDHAM, 1½ miles from Center, and two from Willimantic; good house, barn, &c.; variety of young fruit; stock and tools for sale.

175 acres,	No. 4028,	$5,000

In BOLTON, three miles from depot, three-fourths from school, and twelve miles from Hartford; twenty acres of heavy timber, and fifty acres of lighter growth of wood; three fruit orchards; mowing and tillage smooth, uses machines, well divided and watered; excellent two story house with L, wood house, shop, and hog house attached, painted white; barn 30 x 40; water at the house and yards; stock and tools for sale.

51 acres,	No. 4029,	$5,000

In SOUTH WINDSOR, one-fourth mile from school and church, but eight miles from Hartford, and two miles from rail road station; three acres young woodland; nice orchard of choice fruit; balance well divided and watered, and under high cultivation; has a two story brick house with L, new tobacco sheds; new barn 30 x 40, with cellar, horse barn 20 x 30; cuts over twenty tons of hay; front door-yard fence painted white, &c., a bargain.

131 acres,   No. 4033, $12,000

IN WEST CROMWELL, near rail road station, five miles from the city of Meriden and Middletown, five from New Britain, and twelve from Hartford; is a splendid stock farm; *cuts over seventy-five tons of hay;* three acres of orcharding; twenty acres natural mowing; cuts very heavy grass, and first quality; twenty acres A 1 tobacco land; lands smooth, uses machine; seven acres of wood and timber; land is well fenced and watered; location pleasant, near school, railroad station, &c.; excellent buildings, two story and L house, two new barns with basements, carriage house, granary, &c.

125 acres,   No. 4036, $1,800

IN EAST GLASTENBURY, near school, three miles from church, &c.; seven acres wood and timber; $1\frac{1}{2}$ acres of orcharding, select fruit; two acres of orcharding, rather old; keeps fifteen head of stock; two story and L house, new barn, two cow houses, &c.; terms easy.

130 acres,   No. 4037, $2,500

IN SCOTLAND; thirty acres to wood, *which will pay for the farm;* balance suitably divided; located within one mile of Boston & Erie Rail Road, now being built; near school, saw mill, grist mill, and seed mill; has a good $1\frac{1}{2}$ story house, two good barns, and other buildings; has an excellent water privilege; stock and tools for sale.

12 acres,   No. 4038, $5,000

IN ELLINGTON; land very choice; orchard of select fruits; main house 50 x 40, four story, with two wings, each 32 x 40, three story, containing forty-six rooms; pure spring water brought into the house by aqueduct, and never fails; grounds handsomely adorned with evergreens, hedge fences &c.; for school purposes, a private or public hospital, or a summer boarding house, it is unequalled by anything in the country; the buildings alone cost $10,000; terms easy.

5 acres,   No. 4041, $400

IN NORTH COVENTRY, two miles from Pomroy's Hotel; a nearly new $1\frac{1}{2}$ story house and a small barn; has some fruit; good well and a fine spring near the door; terms, $200 cash; balance, $50 a year.

20 acres, mills, &c.,   No. 4043, $5,500

IN CHAPLIN; splendid water privilege, with forty-two feet fall; heavy stone dam; saw mill, grist mill, &c.; running gear and wheels nearly new; $1\frac{1}{2}$ story dwelling house, painted white, new barn, with basement, sheds, &c.

140 acres,   No. 4044, $8,000

IN WEST NORFOLK; land suitably divided; abundance of timber and wood, will cut 500 cords; fine grove of fifty sugar-maples; large variety of choice fruit; located on a turnpike road, one mile out, near mills, &c., and four miles from Canaan Depot; good house with L, in fine order, two large barns, carriage house, horse barn and shed, all painted white, and in prime order; door-yard fence, twelve rods long, set on stone posts; shade trees, &c.; location pleasant and desirable.

120 acres,	No. 4051,	$10,000

In DURHAM, within one-fourth mile of school, one-half mile of church, near post office, &c.; land is of the first quality, well divided and well fenced; young orcharding, wood-land, &c.; two story and L house, painted white, barn 30 x 40, with basement, granary, &c.; pleasantly located, 5½ miles from the city of Middletown.

19 acres,	No. 4053,	$2,200

In FARMINGTON, seven miles from Hartford, land suitable for tobacco or any crop; two acres of muck, twelve feet deep; has a young fruit orchard, good well of water, and a good brook running through the farm; has a new two story house, painted; new barn with basement; located two miles from Farmington, and two from West Hartford.

90 acres,	No. 4058,	$16,000

In BLOOMFIELD, five miles from Hartford; excellent tobacco land, considerable wood and fruit; land is well watered and divided; water in the house; has a good two story and L house, suitable for two families; three barns, tobacco shed, and cider mill: location one-half mile from the Center

20 acres,	No. 4059,	$3,500

In BLOOMFIELD, located directly opposite No. 4058; excellent land; has an old style house, not very good; no other buildings; will be sold with No. 4058 if desired.

145 acres,	No. 4230,	$9,000

In FARMINGTON, 6 miles west of State House; 4½ miles from Hartford city limits; 2½ miles from Farmington Center; land all lies in a body, and is a fine tobacco or milk farm; has a variety of fruit, &c.; large, 2 story, pleasant and convenient house, painted white; 2 barns, and other convenient out-buildings; land is well watered and fenced; located directly on Farmington Avenue.

Offered *for sale low, to close an estate.* Terms easy.

96 acres,	No. 4061,	$2,000

In MARLBORO, 2½ miles from the Center; 1 mile from village, store, post-office, factories, &c.; 25 acres woodland; 8 acres quite heavy timber;

4 acre lot, perfectly smooth ; remainder somewhat uneven and stony ; plenty of fruits ; has a 1½ story house ; barn, 25 ⋈ 35, with basement ; horse barn, hog house, wood and wagon house, &c. Terms 2-3 cash.

80 acres, No. 4062, $4,000

In WINTHROP, town of Saybrook ; 5 miles from sea shore and depot at Westbrook ; three from Connecticut river steamboat landing ; has 25 acres heavy white oak and hickory timber ; abundance of fruits ; 2 story and L house ; nice barn, carriage room, &c. ; good well of water at the house and one in the barn ; well located ; only ½ mile from school and Baptist church. Terms ½ cash.

ALSO, FOR SALE, 1-3 interest in a capital water privilege, saw and shingle mill, near the farm.

150 acres, No. 4065, $7,500

In BUCKLAND, ¼ mile from railroad station, in the town of Manchester ; 18 acres to wood, ½ heavy timber ; farm lies on Hockanum river ; well divided ; natural mowing, tillage and pasturing ; choice tobacco land ; well fenced and watered ; nice young orchard, 150 trees, just beginning to bear ; has an excellent 1½ story house, painted white and blinded ; pump in the house from a well ; one large barn, granary, carriage house, &c. ; ½ mile from school, and 6 miles from Hartford ; stock and tools for sale if wanted.

21 acres, No. 4066, $4,000

In SOMERS, near by academy, churches, post-office, &c. ; nice brick house with L, painted white and blinded ; good well and cistern ; barn, 36 ⋈ 36 ; carriage house, granary, wood house, tobacco shed, 24 ⋈ 24 ; soil, A, No. 1 ; 1½ acres covered with choice kinds of fruits ; front picket fence, with stone posts ; fine row of sugar maples in front ; will sell a part or the whole.

43 acres, No. 4070, $7,500

In BLOOMFIELD, ½ mile from centre ; all tillable land ; has some wood and young fruit trees ; well watered and fenced ; water at the house and barn ; 2 story and L house, painted white and blinded ; 2 barns, &c. ; located 5 miles from Hartford.

6 acres, No. 4071, $1,100

In GRANBY ; choice land ; 2 story and L house ; barn, with 3 good stalls ; an old shop, &c. ; good cistern water ; located near the centre. Terms, $750 cash.

1 acre, Hotel, Stable, &c.,   No. 4076, $3,500

ON CONNECTICUT RIVER, in an enterprising village; large 2 story building; contains 20 rooms and a large Masonic hall; water in the hotel; cook range, &c.; has a nice barn, with basement, containing 18 stalls; has one acre choice land in garden; mail routes and stages center at the hotel; will sell the entire property, with furniture and fixtures, horses, omnibuses, carriage, sleighs, &c., &c., for $5,000, or as above.

300 acres,   No. 4078, $8,000

IN NORTH GRANBY, ¾ mile from school and 1 from post-office; 5 from railroad depot; plenty of wood; well fenced and watered; orcharding will produce $1,000 worth of choice fruit in a good season; farm will keep 30 head of stock; has two, 2 story houses, 28 × 36, painted white; large barn, store houses, horse sheds, &c.; also, a 1½ story house, with a wood house, a good large barn, with basement; well located, and can be well divided into three good farms, with suitable buildings for each.

64 acres,   No. 4084, $4,750

IN SAG HARBOR, on Long Island; land choice and productive; well divided, and suited to the culture of garden or field crops; is well stocked with apple, pear, peach and quince trees, grape vines, &c.; soil varies from a clay to a sandy loam; is easily worked, and *free from stone;* 2 story house, with spring water by aqueduct; barn, 36 × 40; sheds, &c.; buildings all nearly new; plenty of wood, and a fine clay bed.

50 acres,   No. 4088, $1,000

IN MANSFIELD; land suitably divided into mowing, pasturage and woodland; has a good meadow for the cranberry culture; good fruits, &c.; good house, barn, wagon house and wood shed; location, one mile from church and post-office.

150 acres,   No. 4091, $5,000

IN SIMSBURY, near Tariffville; land well watered and finely fenced; A, 1 tobacco land; 30 acres natural mowing; 20 acres heavy wood and timber; located a short distance from railroad depot; one mile from district and graded schools; 4 churches, post-office, &c.; 14 miles from Hartford; land is smooth, uses machines; 2 story and L house, painted white; milk and ice house, 2 barns, a splendid large tobacco barn, 25 × 85, 2 story and basement, nicely covered and painted white; good wells, cistern, with pump, &c.; will sell stock and tools, if desired. Terms easy.

46 acres,   No. 4092, $2,500

IN SOUTH WINDSOR, ¼ mile from school, 1¼ from church, 4½ from Rockville and 11 from Hartford; has a good old style house, 2 very good barns and carriage sheds; aqueduct water in the house; 6 acres to wood, 5 acres natural mowing; balance, tillage and pasturage; can be had with stock, tools, &c.

70 acres,   No. 4094, $8,000

IN WEST HARTFORD, near Trout Brook Reservoir: land suitably divided; 2 story house, old style; 2 barns and cow sheds, granary, wood and carriage house; 2 good wells, some wood, and fruit. Buildings in fair order.

130 acres,   No. 4096, $2,000

IN HEBRON, 2 miles from center. *Wood enough on the farm to pay for it.* Considerable fruit; cranberry bog, &c.; mowing and tillages are smooth; good stock and grain farm; dwelling house and barn; located ½ mile from school and Methodist church; 4 factories, &c. Terms $1,500 cash. Will exchange.

130 acres,   No. 4097, $6,000

IN BERLIN, near railroad station, 3 miles from New Britain and 9 from Hartford; 25 acres to wood, 10 acres of orcharding; land is smooth, choice for tobacco; will keep 20 cows and other stock; 2 story house, large barn, granary and sheds. Stock and tools for sale.

41 acres,   No. 4099, $6,700

IN BLOOMFIELD, ½ mile from the center; land is choice; excellent mowing, tillage and pasture, and fine orcharding; 2 story and L house, painted and blinded; front picket fence; barn, 36 × 40; tobacco barn, 24 × 76; shed, 40 feet long; well located; only 5½ miles out of Hartford.

240 acres,   No. 4101, $4,000

IN WILLIMANTIC, 2 miles from the center; over 75 acres wood and timber; land well watered, fenced and divided; excellent stock farm; 2 story and L house, painted white and blinded; 2 barns; sheds, granary, wood and well house. *Wood and timber alone will pay for the farm and the expense of getting it off.* Stock and tools if wanted. We offer *a great bargain,* less than 17 *dollars per acre, including buildings.*

12 acres,   No. 4102, $1,300

IN ENFIELD, 1 mile from Hazardville; land is a light, loamy soil; 1½ story house, painted white and blinded; good well of pure, soft water;

barn, 20 ⋈ 24 ; carriage shed and workshop ; young fruit orchard in bearing ; located near church, school and post-office ; only 1 mile from the Shaker Village.

8 acres,   No. 4103, $6,500

On Vine Street, Hartford : choice land for early gardening ; well stocked with choice varieties of fruit, trees, vines, etc. ; good 2 story and L house, barn and sheds.

43 acres,   No. 4104, $6,500

In Enfield, 2½ miles from Thompsonville, and midway between Springfield and Hartford ; all choice tillable land for tobacco, fruit, or early gardening ; 140 apple trees, 40 in bearing ; pears, quinces, grapes, etc. ; 1 story and L house, blinded ; barn, 30 ⋈ 50, with basement ; 2 tobacco sheds, etc.; located ½ mile east of Connecticut river.   Terms, half cash.   Stock and tools for sale.

8 acres,   No. 4106, $4,000

In West Hartford, 20 minutes drive from the city ; large amount of select fruit in full bearing ; excellent land for any crop ; good brick house ; nice new barn, with basement; *desirable property, and cheap.*

250 acres,   No. 4108, $5,000

In Hampton ; 75 acres heavy timber and wood ; on the line of the New Boston and Erie Railroad ; *wood and timber will pay for the farm* ; one of the best stock, grain and fruit farms in the county, orcharding usually producing over 1,000 bushels of select fruit ; excellent 2 story and L house ; 2 barns ; sheds, etc. ; near by school and good neighbors ; 6 miles from Willimantic ; farm is splendidly fenced and well watered ; stock and tools may be had with the farm.

30 acres,   No. 4109, $5,000

In South Windsor, 1¼ mile from rail road station ; excellent tobacco land ; sixty choice fruit trees, vines, small fruits, &c. ; one good dwelling house and one old one ; aqueduct water in house and barn ; barn 24 x 33, tobacco shed 24 x 30, carriage and wood house, and shed ; located eight miles east of Hartford.

150 acres,   No. 4110, $3,500

In Bolton, about twelve miles from Hartford ; forty acres young woodland ; 350 fruit trees, 150 of choice grafted fruit ; good two story and L house with wood and hog house attached, all painted white and blinded ; two barns, with aqueduct water from spring, cow shed fifty feet long, front picket fence, painted ; farm is under good cultivation, and *offered cheap.*

61 acres,   No. 4111, $4,200

In Farmington, three miles from Farmington and West Hartford Center, five from New Britain; good tobacco or stock farm; some fruit; land somewhat uneven and stony, well fenced and watered; located three-fourths mile from school.

7 acres,   No. 4112, $2,500

In Simsbury, two miles from Hop Meadow, one-third mile of school; all choice land; variety of select fruit; nice two story and L house, good barn with basement, large shed, &c.

47 acres,   No. 4113, $3,000

In Berlin, 2½ miles from Berlin Center, one-half mile from rail road station, near school, mills, &c.; five acres of woodland; balance well divided, with choice land for gardening, or any crop; 250 young and thrifty fruit trees; a never-failing stream runs through the farm; good comfortable old style dwelling house, barn with basement; land rather uneven, *but not stony*.

140 acres,   No. 4115, $4,000

In Windham, two miles from Center, one mile from church, one-half mile from school and mills, one mile from proposed depot of B. H. & E. R. R., now being built; excellent farm house painted white, two good barns, one with a fine basement, and the other easily made so; choice mowing and tillage; large amount of orcharding; thirty acres of woodland; farm is well fenced, and watered by never failing streams and springs.

180 acres,   No. 4116, $4,500

In Bolton, within fifty rods of school, 2½ miles from Bolton Center, four miles from Cheneyville, and but twelve from Hartford; land well divided, watered, and fenced; *cuts fifty tons of hay*, mostly by machine; thirty acres to wood; plenty of fruit. &c.; good 1½ story and L house, with wood house painted and blinded, two large barns, with cellar, and painted; good wells at house and barn; 150 acres, with the buildings, may be had for $4,000: twenty five head of stock, and tools, for sale.

33 acres,   No. 4118, $6,000

Village Residence and farm, in Windham Center; thirty-three acres of choice land, located on both sides of Main St.; two sets of buildings; will be sold together, or in two parcels; eleven acres with large mansion house, barn, wood shed, &c., with aqueduct water in the house, from spring, for $3,000; balance of twenty-two acres, located opposite, with two dwellings, barn, choice fruit, &c., $3,000; *must be sold to close an estate*.

2

56 acres,   No. 4121, $2,600

In BRISTOL, one mile from depot; farm is evenly divided into woodland, mowing, tillage, and pasturage; considerable choice fruit; good two story house with L, painted white and blinded; barn, sheds, &c.

160 acres,   No. 4122, $2,600

In HEBRON, Gilead society; excellent farm, well fenced and watered, and evenly divided; a fine never failing stream runs through the farm; will summer and winter twenty-five head of stock; good two story and L house painted; good barn and other buildings; plenty of wood; will sell a part, or the whole, on easy terms; also for sale, near the above, A GOOD FARM FOR $2,500.

50 acres,   No. 4123, $1,200

In TOLLAND, pleasantly located, within five miles of Rockville, near school, saw and grist mill, &c.; farm is well divided into mowing, tillage, pasture, and woodland; house, barn, wood house, &c., all in good order.

165 acres,   No. 4124, $5,000

In TOLLAND, only 4½ miles from Rockville; beautiful and desirable location, and one of the best farms in town; twenty acres woodland: young orchard of seventy-five trees; aqueduct water to the barn; land choice and smooth, uses machines; nice two story and L house, painted white and blinded; a very fine new barn, 40 x 60, with basement under the whole, painted, &c.; located three miles from Tolland and Wellington depot; stock and tools for sale.

150 acres,   No. 4125, $2,500

In WEST GRANVILLE, Mass.; thirty acres timber and woodland; 200 young and thrifty grafted fruit trees, besides plenty of fruit in bearing; well fenced, and watered by streams and springs; excellent stock farm; located one-half mile from school, six miles from Hitchcockville, two from West Hartland, and twelve from Winsted; 1½ story house with L, painted, three good barns, with water in yards; stock and tools for sale.

42 acres,   No. 4127, $2,500

In FARMINGTON, one-fourth mile from rail road station; excellent orcharding, some woodland; raises choice tobacco; new 1½ story house, new barn, 16 x 24.

73 acres,   No. 4128, $6,500
70 acres,   No. 4128, $6,000
28 acres,   No. 4128, $3,800

In BERLIN, pleasantly situated, one-half mile from church, store, post office, &c., in the center; two dwellings, two barns; land very choice; two story dwelling house painted white, barn with basement, cow house, &c.; also, 1½ story house with barn; stock, tools, &c., for sale.

50 acres, No. 4130, $3,000

In WHIGVILLE, town of BURLINGTON; located in the village, within one-fourth mile of three churches, school, three factories, &c.; farm is well fenced and under good cultivation; fruit in abundance; has an unimproved water-power of twenty feet fall; two story and L house, painted, one good barn and one old one, wagon shop, cow houses, &c., supplied with aqueduct water; stock and tools for sale; terms easy.

50 acres, No. 4131, $1,700

In SOUTH MANCHESTER, 2½ miles from Cheneyville, 1½ miles from rail road station; has some wood, considerable fruit; choice tobacco land; good 1½ story house, and good barn; ten miles from Hartford; stock and tools for sale.

65 acres, No. 4132, $2,000

In WEST GRANBY; five acres of woodland, large orchard, &c.; 1½ story house, one good barn, cider mill and distillery; will exchange for a smaller place near school, &c.

60 acres, No. 4134, $800

In TOLLAND; land suitably divided into woodland, pasture, and tillage; *the wood on the farm alone will pay for it.*

54 acres, mills, &c., No. 4135, $1,850

In TOLLAND, has a good SAW AND SHINGLE MILL, splendid CIDER MILL, all run by water power; good house, barn, and other buildings; land divided into mowing, tillage, pasture, and wood, with a good supply of fruit; has two excellent water privileges; will sell the mills and nine acres for $1,100.

100 acres, No. 4137, $5,000

In CROMWELL, splendidly located on the Hartford and Middletown turn-pike; choice land for tobacco or gardening; smooth and level, *entirely free from stone;* post and rail fence; twenty acres of wood and timber; two old orchards, and fifty fine thrifty young apple trees, sixty dwarf and standard pear trees, cherries, grapes, and small fruits; good two story house, painted white; two barns, and sheds; five miles from Middletown and ten from Hartford; stock and tools if wanted.

45 acres, No. 4138, $2,700

In EAST WINDSOR; five acres of wood; balance well divided, no waste land; watered by streams and springs; choice tobacco land twenty-five fruit trees; good two story brick house, wood shed, and well house, barn quite poor; choice meadow land; located one-half mile from school and church, five from Rockville, and eleven from Hartford.

47 acres, mills, &c.,   No. 4139, $2,500

In HEBRON, four miles from Andover depot, one-fourth mile from school, one-half mile from churches, &c.; has a grist mill and water privilege; mill in good running order, with plenty of custom; two run of stone, corn and cob cracker, &c.; eight acres of wood, and three acres in orcharding; 1½ story house, painted, barn 24 x 48, with aqueduct water, wood house, wagon shed, hog house, etc.; terms one-half cash.

120 acres,   No. 4141, $2,300

In BURLINGTON, two miles from Center, three from Harwinton, eighteen from Hartford; land well divided into mowing, tillage, pasture, and wood; near by school, factory, saw mill, etc.; some fruit; fences are good; will summer and winter fifteen head of stock.

142 acres,   No. 4143, $2,500

In HEBRON, 1¼ mile from Center; has a new house and barn; land well divided and watered; excellent tillage and pasturage; *wood and timber enough on the farm to pay for it.*

10 acres,   No. 4144, $1,000

In THE VILLAGE of Hope Valley, town of Hebron, near school, factories, etc.; good orchard of fruit, with house, barn, etc.

20 acres,   No. 4145, $1,000

In HEBRON, three miles from Center; variety of fruit; new two story house and barn.

150 acres,   No. 4147, $3,500

In COLLINSVILLE, 2¼ miles from the village, located on the Farmington River; fifty acres is of a fine black loamy soil, twenty acres light sandy soil, and the balance woodland, some of it *heavy timber;* plenty of apples and grapes; aqueduct water at the house and barn; large two story and L house, painted and papered throughout, large barn, two large sheds, granary, carriage house, hog house with boiler set, large barn in one of the back lots, etc.; *a good stock farm and offered low.*

75 acres,   No. 4148, $4,200

In DURHAM, one-half mile from Durham St., schools, churches, stores, post office, etc.; one of the best farms in the town for growth of crops; splendid orchard of seventy-five trees that cannot be surpassed; well divided into mowing, tillage, pasture, and woodland, with excellent house, barn, and outbuildings; desirably located, and offered low, with stock and tools if wanted.

50 acres,   No. 4149, $4,500

In WINDSORVILLE, one-half mile from school, church, post office, factory, etc.; choice land, three acres to wood; excellent pastures, and well watered good young fruit orchard; fences good; water brought to house and barn from spring; large 1½ story and L house in good order, good barn, tobacco shed, wood house, piggery, new granary, etc.; stock and tools may be had with the farm.

50 acres,   No. 4150, $750

In EAST HADDAM, 2¼ miles from Goodspeed's Landing on Connecticut River; divided into mowing, tillage, pasture, and woodland; some fruit; watered by a never failing stream; fenced mostly by stone wall; buildings of little or no value; has a fine view of the mouth of Connecticut River, and the Sound; terms $400 cash.

225 acres,   No. 4151, $10,000

In ELLINGTON, one mile from the Center; buildings nearly new; house 1½ story, painted white and blinded; two barns, tobacco shed, and other buildings; farm is well divided and watered, and very easy to cultivate; well located on the main travelled road, within five miles of Rockville, fifteen from Hartford, and sixteen from Springfield; has a fine peat bed, and an abundance of rich muck deposit; fruit, etc.; terms one-half cash.

21 acres,   No. 4152, $1,500

In ELLINGTON, one mile from the Center, adjoining No. 4151; nice one story house, painted white and blinded, excellent barn, etc.; land good; offered very low; terms one-half cash.

100 acres,   No. 4153, $1,000

In BOLTON, 1¾ miles from Andover depot; sixty acres sprout land; balance tillage, pasture, and woodland; located near school, and good neighbors; no buildings on the farm; terms one-half cash.

90 acres,   No. 4154, $3,500

In ANDOVER, 1½ miles from Andover depot; eight acres to wood and timber; balance mowing, tillage, pasture, and orcharding; has one of the best fruit orchards in town; young, thrifty, and in full bearing; located within one-fourth mile of stores, saw and grist mill, etc.; nice two story house with L, painted white and blinded; good well of water, two good barns, one being new, with basement, etc.; horse barn and granary; terms one-half cash.

80 acres,   No. 4155, $2,000

In WILLINGTON, 1½ miles from Mansfield four corners, near a good market, and convenient distance from three rail road depots; land suitably divided into mowing, tillage, woodland, and pasturage; watered by streams and springs; has a nice young orchard, two story house with L, two barns, wagon house, shed, etc.

215 acres,   No. 4156, $6,000

In HAMPTON, only one mile from the Center; very pleasantly and desirably situated; is a SPLENDID DAIRY AND CROP FARM; will keep twenty cows, two yoke of oxen, one pair of horses, and fifty sheep; has a large nice two story house, a never failing well of pure water, two large barns, with water in each yard, carriage house, granary, etc., all in the best of repair; within one mile of the Center, where are stores, schools, churches, post office, hotel, factories, shops, etc.; one of the *best and cheapest farms in the town.*

100 acres,   No. 4159, $5,000

In VERNON, only one mile from Rockville, two from Vernon depot; sixteen acres to wood; four acres of orcharding; farm lies on Hockanum River; well fenced and watered; has a nice two story and L house, painted white and blinded, two nice barns with basement; aqueduct water to house and barn, with sufficient head to throw water over the barn; half mile from school; terms, half cash. Stock and tools for sale.

90 acres,   No. 4160, $1,800

In WILLINGTON, ¾ mile from Moose Meadow, church, etc.; 4½ from Stafford Springs; 1½ story house, barn, shed and wagon house; good variety of fruits, vines, etc.; cuts 15 tons best quality of hay; pleasantly situated, well watered, plenty of muck; wood and timber enough to bring $3,000 in the market; only 3½ miles from railroad depot.

25 acres,   No. 4161, $3,500

NEAR SOUTHINGTON CENTER; 4 acres to wood; considerable choice fruit; 60 trees been grafted 5 years; land watered by streams and springs; 2 story and L house, painted white; barn, with basement; water in the house and at the barn.

125 acres,   No. 4162, $7,000

In TORRINGTON, 2¾ miles from Wolcottville, one of the best of markets; good supply of wood; farm will keep 30 head of stock; principal part of mowing done by machine; fruit of every variety; one large and nearly new dwelling house and 5 barns, 3 of them recently built, with running water to all; 100 extra Spanish merino ewes, Vermont style, and other stock for sale if wanted.

18 acres,	No. 4163,	$7,500

In WINDSOR, on the Green; 2 story brick house, with hipped roof, stone foundation; can be easily altered into a modern style French roof; pleasantly situated; 10 minutes walk from three churches, schools, post-office and depot; 15 minutes by railroad from Hartford; variety of fruits.

50 acres, store, &c.,	No. 4164,	$15,000

In A THRIVING TOWN; splendidly situated in the center of the place; buildings are new and in order; 30 *acres of the best land in the State, with fine fruit;* balance is excellent pasture, with a fine maple orchard; has a nice, large, new dwelling house, that could not now be built for $10,000; a fine store, with an established trade of $20,000 to $30,000 per year; only 2 hours by rail from Hartford, and four from New York. *We need not add that this is a great bargain.*

100 acres,	No. 4165,	$15,000

In HARTFORD, just over the city line; corner property; 2 story brick house; finely located; 2 barns; land very choice; an A 1 milk farm; will keep 25 cows; will sell the whole, or a part, without the buildings, *very low.* Terms, ½ cash.

150 acres,	No. 4166,	$12,000

ONE half mile from GRANBY CENTER; very choice land; well watered and fenced; 15 acres of wood; splendid meadow; grass cut by machines; fruit in abundance; 2 story and L house, painted white; 2 barns, cider mill, tenant house, etc.; located 17 miles from Hartford, ½ mile from two churches, and 3 from railroad depot.

40 acres,	No. 4167,	$1,300

In BOLTON, ¼ mile from depot; land suitably divided, watered and fenced; free from stone; considerable choice fruit; near by school; located on a turnpike road; 20 acres of woodland, 15 years' growth; good 1½ story house, painted white and blinded; supplied with aqueduct water and a good well; good barn and blacksmith shop, where can be had plenty of custom.

327 acres,	No. 4168,	$8,000
150 acres,	No. 4168,	$5,500

In EAST GLASTENBURY; ½ mile from school; an excellent stock farm; will keep 20 head the year around and 30 head in summer; considerable fruit; 165 acres to wood and timber; 2 story house, painted white and blinded; barn, 2 cow houses and carriage house; will sell the whole, or a part, as above, on easy terms.

| 86 acres, | No. 4169, | $9,000 |
| 36 acres, | No. 4169, | $3,000 |

In BERLIN, just outside of the village; land A No. 1; suitable for tobacco, or any crop; abundance of fruit; 17 acres of woodland; fine sugar maple orchard of 60 trees; new 2 story and L house, painted white and blinded; nice barn, granary and sheds; 2 good tenant houses and barn; will sell the whole, or a part, as above.

| 80 acres, | No. 4170, | $1,200 |

In ANDOVER, 1¾ miles from railroad depot; land well divided; 3 acres heavy timber and considerable of light growth; fruit orchard, etc.; 2 story and L house, in fair order; barn wants covering; possession any time; $700 cash; balance on mortgage to the State school fund.

| 2 acres, | No. 4171, | $4,000 |

In ROCKY HILL, VILLAGE RESIDENCE, and 2 acres of choice land; nice 2 story house with L, painted white and blinded; water in the house and a good well at the door; nice large barn, sheds, granary, horse barn and wood house; fruit of 75 to 100 trees, thrifty and in full bearing; grapes, strawberries, currants, etc.; pleasantly situated near the center of the village; very desirable and cheap.

| 177 acres, | No. 4172, | $2,500 |

In ASHFORD, 1 mile from Pompey Hollow; 30 acres wood and timber, mostly hard wood; balance of farm suitably divided; will keep 18 to 20 head of stock; orcharding of 125 trees; pears, etc.; old style 2 story house in front, 1 story in rear; barn, 30 x 53; sheep house, 22 x 30; granary, carriage house and wood shed.

| 20 acres, | No. 4173, | $3,000 |

In WINDSORVILLE, about 1 mile from the village; nice 1½ story house with 2 L's, painted white and blinded; barn with cellar, painted; horse barn and shed, all nearly new and in perfect order; some fruit; 1 acre of woodland; land well fenced; has a trout brook directly in the rear of the barn; land lies on both sides of the road; new picket fence the entire length of the front and painted white.

| 200 acres, | No. 4174, | $3,000 |

In COLCHESTER, 1¾ miles from the village, where are churches, schools, free academy, stores, post-office, hotel, factories, etc.; 50 acres of woodland, one half of it heavy timber; ¾ mile from saw and grist mill; 2 nice orchards, one in bearing, and a fine nursery of select grafts; large 2 story house with L, painted white; pleasant yard, with hedge fences, walks, etc.; 2 good barns; wood and carriage house; sold to close an estate.

125 acres,   No. 4175, $5,500

In EAST WINDSOR, 4 miles from Rockville; 25 acres of wood and timber, balance well divided; plenty of rich muck deposit; 200 apple trees and other fruits; 1½ story and L house, painted white and blinded; 2 large barns, cow house, wagon house, tobacco sheds, wood and hog house, etc.; more land can be had with the above, if desired, on easy terms.

150 acres,   No. 4176, $2,200

In WINTHROP, pleasantly situated; well watered with streams and springs; *wood and timber will more than twice pay for the farm;* variety of choice fruit; only 4 miles from DEEP RIVER LANDING ON CONNECTICUT RIVER, 5 from sea shore; old style dwelling house; wood and wagon house, barn and shop; $1,100 cash.

170 acres,   No. 4177, $2,800

In CHATHAM, East Hampton Society, 2½ miles from the village; excellent stock farm; cuts 25 tons of upland hay; plenty of grafted fruit; peat and muck; easy of access; well watered by a never-failing stream, on which is a fall of 12 to 14 feet; good sized dwelling; 2 barns, large carriage and wood house; buildings all good; barns nearly new.

40 acres,   No. 4178, $3,500

On COLUMBIA GREEN; excellent land; 2 story and L house, with wood house connected; barn, etc.; all built within five years; 15 acres of woodland, balance well divided; 5 miles from Willimantic, and 4½ from Andover depot; finely located on the village green.

250 acres,   No. 4181, $7,200

In PUTNAM; 50 acres of woodland; balance mowing, tillage and pasture; buildings consist of a capacious house, 3 barns, new granary, sheds and other buildings; land well watered; water in cattle yards; has kept 25 head of cattle the year around for years, and is called *the best farm in town.* *Terms easy.*

30 acres,   No. 4182, $1,700

In NORTH COVENTRY, 1½ miles from the center; 5 acres to wood; young fruit trees, well watered and fenced; 1 story and L house, in fair order; barn, shed and wood house; 2½ miles from depot.

10 acres,   No. 4184,   . $1,700

In WEST HARTFORD, 5 miles from city of Hartford; 10 acres of good land; thrifty young orchard, 14 varieties of select fruit, in bearing; 1½ story house with L, painted white and blinded; barn and wagon shed; all in fair order.

50 acres,   No. 4187, $4,000

In LEBANON, 2¼ miles from Willimantic; 3 acres to wood, balance evenly divided and fenced; nice young fruit orchards, a fair supply in bearing; land smooth and free from stone; 2 dwelling houses; one a 2 story and L, with wood room and shop, painted white; the other a 2 story in front with L, old style house, one story in rear; barn 50 feet long; carriage house and shed; granary and hog house; near school, etc.; $2,000 cash.

75 acres,   No. 4189, $4,000

In BOLTON, 3½ miles from depot, ¼ mile from school, 1 mile from church; 20 acres to wood; balance tillage and pasture; cuts 20 tons of hay by machine; keeps 10 head of stock; stock and tools for sale at a bargain; $2,000 cash.

75 acres,   No. 4190, $20,000

In NEW BRITAIN, 1½ miles from center; all choice land, well watered and fenced; 7 acres of timber and wood; excellent buildings; pleasantly located; near school, etc.; $5,000 cash.

13 acres,   No. 4191, $4,500

Village residence in Forestville, town of Bristol; nice 2 story and L house, painted and blinded; good well and cistern; 2 story barn, painted; 5 minutes walk from depot, schools, church, post-office, etc.; photograph may be seen at this office.

1 acre,   No. 4194, $2,500

In VILLAGE OF CHESTER, on Connecticut river; nearly new 2 story house, Gothic style; new barn, etc.; abundance of young fruit in bearing; will exchange for city property.

16 acres,   No. 4196, $2,500

In BLOOMFIELD, 1¼ miles from center; all choice land; abundance of select fruits; 2 story and L house; barn, carriage house and shop, wagon sheds and hog house; also, a small tenant house; $1,900 cash.

2 acres,   No. 4197, $1,650

ON MANCHESTER GREEN; nearly new 2 story house, in good style and painted white; 100 fruit trees, just beginning to bear; pleasantly situated, 100 rods from the center, and about 15 minutes walk from North Manchester depot; stage to depot every train.

140 acres,   No. 4199, $10,000

IN VERNON CENTER; A SPLENDID FARM; suitably divided; 50 acres of woodland; well watered; splendidly fenced; *every foot can be mowed by machine;* orchard of select fruit; 30 varieties of grapes; aqueduct water in barn; good wells, etc.; 2 story and L house, painted white and blinded; barn 40 x 65; carriage house, ice house, granary, sheds, 2 story shop, etc.; *one of the best farms in the county;* will sell the whole, or any part, with the buildings.

50 acres,   No. 4200, $5,500

IN EAST AVON, two miles from the Center; wood suitable for farm use; well watered and fenced; good supply of fruit, and 200 young trees not in bearing; located on Farmington River; land smooth, uses machines, cuts large amount of good hay; two story and L house, with wood house, painted white, large barn, shed, cider mill and distillery by water power; mill, distillery, and water power for $1,000 extra from price of farm.

82 acres,   No. 4202, $6,000

IN VERNON, only one mile from Rockville, and twelve from Hartford; well located on the main road: some wood and timber, balance all choice land; two story and basement house; aqueduct water in the house and barn; variety of select fruit; wagon house, granary, wood and ice house, and barn; capital water privilege, new dam, twenty-five feet fall; raises choice tobacco and other crops; a very desirable farm, and *offered low.*

4½ acres,   No. 4203, $3,500

IN WEST HARTFORD, about five miles from Hartford; excellent land; two story and L house, barn, tobacco shed, etc.

56 acres,   No. 4204, $9,500

IN PLAINVILLE, three-fourths mile from the Center, one-fourth mile from school; all good land, and suitably divided; three acres to wood; splendid young apple orchard; well fenced and watered; has a splendid building site, which might readily be sold; 1½ story house with basement, painted white and blinded, three good barns, hog house, wood and wagon house, sheds, etc., all in good repair; aqueduct water in the house and cattle yards, never fails; $6,000 cash.

162 acres,   No. 4205, $2,800

IN ASHFORD, 1¼ mile from Center, one mile from church, one-half mile from school; has a one story house painted a straw color, two barns, wood shed, wagon house, granary, hog house, etc.; thirty acres of timber and wood, balance well divided, watered, and fenced; land level, and free from stone; mowing done by machine; no waste land; over 100 grafted fruit trees.

140 acres,   **No. 4206,**   **$2,500**

IN TOLLAND, two miles from Center, and three from Stafford Springs Depot; fifty acres woodland, balance mowing, tillage, and pasture; well watered: has some fruit; 1½ story house with L, two barns, granary, wood and carriage house, etc.; farm is under good cultivation, and keeps fifteen head of stock the year around; $1,500 cash.

1 acre and hotel,   **No, 4208,**   **$4,500**

IN PORTLAND, near Gildersleeve's ship yard, on Connecticut River, opposite the city of Middletown, about forty rods from steamboat wharf; suitable as a desirable place for a PRIVATE RESIDENCE, with a fine view of Connecticut River; or, for a PUBLIC HOUSE; large two story house with a fine basement, painted white and blinded, in first-class order; good well and cistern, with pumps, good barn, new shed 17 x 27; land is choice for gardening; orcharding of select fruits, in variety; terms easy.

65 acres,   **No. 4209,**   **$3,400**

IN SOUTHINGTON, two miles from Plainville, near school, and good neighbors; nine acres of wood, balance evenly divided, well fenced and watered; variety of grafted fruit; land good; two story and L house, two barns, etc.; buildings in fair order; house painted white and blinded; terms two-thirds cash.

37 acres,   **No. 4210,**   **$1,000**

IN SCOTLAND, 2½ miles from Center; good land; suitably divided; has some fruit; 1½ story house, newly covered and painted, two small barns, two sheds, etc.

63 acres,   **No. 4211,**   **$7,000**

IN WEST HARTFORD; ten acres to wood, balance choice land, well watered and fenced; large supply of fruit; seventy-five trees in bearing, and 100 small trees; large old style house in good order, two good wells and cistern, tobacco house with a basement, barn, wood house, granary, etc.; one of the best farms in that section; $5,000 cash.

70 acres,   **No. 4212,**   **$1,000**

IN HEBRON, two miles from Village Green, one mile from factories, near school, etc.; formerly an excellent farm, but has been somewhat neglected of late; has a comfortable house, good barn 30 x 70, covered with pine.

100 acres,   **No. 4214,**   **$8,000**

IN NEW BRITAIN, 1¾ miles from Center, one-half mile from school, three-fourths mile from rail road station; excellent stock farm; considerable scattering wood and timber; well divided, and watered by three streams and two springs; keeps fifteen to twenty head of stock; considerable choice fruit; nice new two story house with nine rooms, painted white and blinded, barn, cider mill, etc.; $3,600 cash.

| 150 acres, | No. 4217, | $2,200 |

In HAMPTON, about six miles from Willimantic, on the main travelled road; twenty-five acres of wood and timber; considerable fruit; 1¼ story house, barn, sheds, etc.; terms easy.

| 150 acres, hotel & store, | No. 4218, | $4,000 |

In ASHFORD; 150 acres of good land, suitably divided; thirty acres to wood; two story and L house, recently painted and blinded; barns and sheds, in good repair; water in the house; 200 select fruit trees from three to six years old; artificial fish pond about thirty rods from the door.

| 185 acres, | No. 4220, | $10,000 |

In WINDSORVILLE; buildings and four acres, located in the center of the village, which will be sold for $4,000; 70 acres, well divided, for $3,000; 150 acres, wood and pasture, one mile distant, $3,000; has a two story house formerly used as a hotel, painted and blinded, two large barns, carriage and wood house, etc.

| 100 acres, | No. 4221, | $4,000 |

In EAST HAMPTON, on EAST HAMPTON LAKE, near by church, school, stores, post office, etc.; latest survey of B. & N. Y. R. R. runs across a piece of land making into the Lake; bounded nearly one-half mile on the Lake; is one of the pleasantest country residences in the State; land is suitably divided into mowing, pasture, and woodland, and well stocked with old and young fruit trees; a large two story house, two barns, carriage and tobacco house; seventy-five acres wood and timber land can be bought with the farm if desired; offered for sale wholly on account of ill health of the owner, *and at a bargain.*

| 162 acres, | No. 4224, | $10,000 |

In WETHERSFIELD, Newington Society, near by school, etc.; land well watered, fences good; two acres of orcharding, select fruits; over 1,000 cords of wood; keeps thirty head of stock; two story house, painted white and blinded, two large barns, sheds, ice house, and a 1½ story tenant house, all in good order, built six years ago.

| 205 acres, shops, &c., | No. 4226, | $8,000 |

In HEBRON, 2½ miles from Center, and 3½ from Colchester; over 3,000 cords of wood on the farm; orcharding of eight acres choice grafted fruit; excellent water privilege, with two good shops; machinery for wood turning, such as lathes, planers, etc.; large two story and L house, for two families, painted white, two barns, carriage house, etc.; $4,000 cash.

1½ acres,   No. 4227, $500

IN BOLTON, one fourth mile from the depot; one story house, barn, shed, etc.; 1½ acres of land, and some fruit; one-fourth mile from school.

150 acres,   No. 4228, $7,500

IN WEST SUFFIELD, 1¼ miles from the Center; splendid stock farm; keeps thirty-five to forty head of stock the year around; ten acres to wood, balance, choice land, well located, and suitably divided; two young fruit orchards; nearly new two story house, painted, barn 35 x 45, with basement, horse barn, wagon house, sheds, milk house, ice house, etc.; also, two story house, barn, and tobacco house, rather old, with good barn; located four miles from Southwick depot, and seven from Windsor Locks

55 acres,   No. 4231, $7,500

IN ROCKY HILL, near the center of the town; splendid land; over 1,000 young fruit trees; two good barns; dwelling house burned in 1864; has a valuable bed of Britannia grit; formerly owned by Gen. James T. Pratt.

105 acres,   No. 4,232, $2,400

IN TOLLAND, 2½ miles from Rockville, two miles from Tolland street, 1½ mile from school; pleasantly located, near good neighbors; forty acres of woodland, balance well divided, watered, and fenced; thrifty orchard of fruit, mostly young and in full bearing; buildings are all new: 1½ story and L house, painted white, barn 35 x 35, with basement, sheds, etc.; will sell seventy-five acres and buildings for $1,800; *a fine farm, and offered very low.*

15 acres,   No. 4233, $8,000

IN WINDSOR LOCKS, on Main street; large 3 story house with L, painted and blinded; good well; 2 good barns, all in good order; variety of fruits; nice grove on the premises, with a never failing stream running through it; ½ mile from school, church, etc.; 30 acres of excellent mowing and tillage can be had with the above if wanted; $4,000 cash.

200 acres,   No. 4234, $50 per acre.

IN HARWINTON; 12 acres heavy timber and wood, 20 acres light growth, 25 to 30 years; 40 acres of mowing and tillage; good pastures; well watered; running stream in the yards; young fruit orchard of 10 acres, just beginning to bear; pleasantly located, on high ground, 3 miles from Harwinton Center and 2 from railroad depot; 1½ story house with L; 3 barns, horse barn, 2 sheds, and small tenant house and barn; will sell 100 acres and buildings, if wanted; terms half cash.

100 acres,	No. 4235,	$2,700

In ANDOVER, 5 minutes walk from depot; 1½ story and L house, painted white; good barn, wood and wagon house, all nearly new; good wells, and aqueduct water in house and barn; splendid water privilege on the farm.

167 acres,	No. 4236,	$3,000

In COLCHESTER, Westchester society, 4 miles from East Hampton Center, 4½ from Connecticut river, 13½ from Middletown, and 20 from Hartford; pleasantly located; ½ mile from school; plenty of wood and timber; considerable fruit; evenly divided, well watered and fenced; capital stock and grain farm; large 2 story house, painted white and blinded, and in good order, with water in the house; 2 barns; wood shed 50 feet long; a very desirable farm, and offered at *a bargain, on easy terms.*

115 acres,	No. 4237,	$8,500

In SOUTHINGTON, ½ mile from school, 2 miles from the center of two villages, where are churches, schools, post-office and depot; buildings in good repair; 2 story and L house, painted white; wood and wagon house, 3 barns, hog house, etc.; 20 acres to wood and timber, ¼ of it heavy chestnut timber; 2 acres of young and old orchards; 75 acres of mowing and tillage; cuts from 40 to 50 tons of hay by machine; good pastures; land well watered by streams, etc.

125 acres,	No. 4238,	$7,000

In WEST ASHFORD, ½ mile from post-office, 5½ from Willington depot, and 12 from Willimantic; 2 story and L house, nearly new and painted white; large barn, shop, etc.; abundance of fruit; wood and timber land; under good cultivation; well divided and fenced.

375 acres,	No. 4239,	$4,000

In WEST ASHFORD; 100 acres of woodland; balance tillage, mowing and pasturage; well watered and fenced; keeps 25 head of cattle, horse, etc.; new 1 story cottage house, with L 44 feet long, painted white, main house blinded; 2 barns, granary, carriage house, shed, etc.; has a good house and an old barn for tenants; good cranberry marsh of 12 acres, produced 20 bushels this year and not cultivated at all; terms easy.

1 acre,	No. 4240,	only $600

In TOLLAND, a few rods from school, ¾ mile from center of town, and but 4 miles from Rockville; fine young orchard, just commencing to bear; beautiful row of shade trees in front; $400 cash; *a bargain.*

100 acres,   No. 4241, $3,000

In WINDHAM, 3 miles from the center; excellent stock farm, splendidly fenced and watered; aqueduct water to yards; fine fruit orchard in bearing; plenty of wood and timber; large 2 story house with L and carriage house, painted white and blinded; 2 large barns; pleasantly located; near by school, saw and grist mill, etc.

150 acres,   No. 4242, $14,000

In HARTFORD, just outside the city limits; an A No. 1 milk farm; orcharding; 2 story brick house; 2 barns, etc., etc.; $7,000 cash.

20 acres,   No. 4243, $4,000

On MANCHESTER GREEN; nice 2 story house with L, painted white and blinded; barn, sheds, etc.; front picket fence and shade trees about the house; all choice land; has some fruit; terms easy.

200 acres,   No. 4244, $7,000

In CANTON; one of the best stock farms in the State; 60 acres of mowing and tillage, 20 of timber, balance pasturage; good 2 story and L farm house; 3 stock barns, sheep house, horse barn, tobacco barn and sheds; running water to the house and barn; keeps about 25 head of cattle in winter and 55 in summer, a pair of horses, sheep, etc.; stock and tools for sale; $5,000 cash; *offered at a bargain.*

3 acres,   No. 4245, $6,000

In CITY OF HARTFORD, on Wethersfield avenue; a splendid building site, comprising about 3 acres of choice land; good fruit orchard; a splendid property for a profitable investment; only $1,500 cash; also, a valuable property on Main street, Hartford; corner property lot, 217 x 580 feet; excellent house, 2 barns, carriage house, sheds, etc.; variety of choice fruits; price $14,500; will sell the buildings with a corner lot, 108 x 290 feet, for $7,500, or will dispose of the land alone at a price which cannot fail to prove a profitable investment.

170 acres,   No. 4246, $12,000

In WOODSTOCK, Windham county; one of the best stock and fruit farms in the State; 20 acres of hard wood and timber; one of the finest apple orchards, thrifty and in full bearing, cannot be surpassed, and a young orchard in partial bearing; cuts about 100 tons of hay of the first quality by machine; has a fine large peat meadow, drained in squares, in mowing; has an inexhaustable supply of muck deposit; 2 story house, 41 x 33, L, 30 x 20, painted and blinded; one barn, 75 x 33, with shed, 30 x 16, with hay-loft; one barn, 30 x 40, with shed, 40 x 14, with hay-loft; basements under each barn; also, a small barn and corn crib, work shop, swill room and set kettle

in cellar, hen house, etc., all in good order; fences are stone and in good
condition; good well at the house, a never failing spring at the barns;
water carried to both barns and swill house from a reservoir; an orchard of
500 pear trees, choice varieties, standard and dwarf; on the farm is a fine
herd of thorough bred Alderney cattle, grades and native stock; a full stock
of machines, tools, steaming apparatus, wagons, carts, and everything necessary for the farm can be purchased low, by any one who buys the farm; land
slopes to the south and east; located ½ mile from church, academy, post-
office, young ladies' seminary, etc., etc.

30 acres, grist mill, &c.,   No. 4247, $3,000

In BROOKLYN; good saw, shingle and grist mill, all in first class running
order; fine water power, capable of running a large mill or factory; 10
acres of wood-land; balance tillage and pasture; good 2 story house, 30 ×
40; barn with 2 sheds attached for stalls; water at the house and barn;
$1,800 cash.

130 acres,   No. 4248, $2,600

In CHAPLIN; farm contains probably 150 acres; heavily timbered and
wooded, enough to pay for the farm; ½ mile from saw and shingle mill, 5
from Willimantic; 2 story house, 2 barns, sheds, etc.; must be sold and
offered low.

20 acres,   No. 4249, $3,000

In HAMPTON, Goshen Society, known as the Newton Clark Estate;
excellent buildings; beautifully located; water brought into the house, up
stairs and down, by aqueduct; excellent out buildings; 3 acres of woodland; splendid garden; choice fruits in abundance; the house alone cost
$4,000. The whole offered for $3,000 to close an estate.

160 acres,   No. 4250, $2,100

In ASHFORD, 1¼ mile from village, church, saw and grist mill, shops,
post-office, stores, etc., and a few rods from school; well divided, plenty of
wood and timber, well watered, and a good supply of fruit; large and convenient house, 2 barns, sheep house, granary, sheds and workshop; water
in the house and both cattle yards; $1,500 cash.

100 acres,   No. 4251, $15,000

In POMFRET, known as the Thurber Farm; one of the best stock farms,
with the finest set of buildings in the State; 30 acres of mowing and tillage,
30 of timber and wood, 40 of pasture and orchard; fenced with heavy
double faced stone wall; land under-drained and well watered; on high
ground; commands an extensive view.

3

70 acres,	No. 4252,	$2,200

In WOODSTOCK VALLEY; 7 acres to wood, 30 acres of mowing and tillage, 5 acres of meadow which abounds in rich muck, balance, pasture; watered with never failing springs and streams; all fenced with stone wall; 100 fruit trees, mostly grafted; good farm house of 11 rooms; barn, wood, carriage and cart house; within 1 mile of store, post-office, grist mill, saw mills, shops, etc.; $1,200 cash.

74 acres,	No. 4253,	$5,000

In COLCHESTER; 30 acres to wood; 100 apple trees, young and choice fruit; well located; ¼ mile from school and church; large 2 story house, and a farm house with 8 rooms; 2 barns, carriage, wagon house and sheds, corn house, tool house; buildings all painted; map of property may be seen at this office.

About 2 acres,	No. 4254,	$3,500

In PORTLAND; fine village residence; nice buildings and choice land; well stocked with variety of choice fruits; offered very low.

130 acres,	No. 4255,	$3,300

In SCOTLAND, 1½ mile from the Center; good 2 story house with L, painted and blinded; barn, sheds, corn and wood house; land well watered; evenly divided; 30 acres of wood and timber; fine young orchard in bearing; conveniently located to church, schools, grist mills, saw mill, etc.; very desirable property and offered low, on account of old age of the owner and inability to carry it on; terms easy.

140 acres, mill, &c.,	No. 4256,	$12,000
40 acres, mill, &c.,	No. 4256,	$6,000
Mill and privilege,	No. 4256,	$4,000

140 acres suitably divided to wood and timber, etc. Large and convenient house, tenant house, barns, saw mill and valuable water privilege, about 20 feet fall; some of the timber very heavy; has a valuable bed of clay, the only one in town; being located in the center of a thriving manufacturing village, renders it very valuable to any one manufacturing brick, which can be made to pay for the property.

90 acres,	No. 4257,	$6,000

In SOUTHAMPTON, Long Island, N. Y.; located on the turnpike, 1½ miles from Sag Harbor; well divided and watered; soil principally a sandy loam; young apple orchard; 1½ story house, water in the kitchen; barn, carriage house, granary, tool house, milk house, hog and hen house, etc.;

has an abundance of clay, suitable for manufacturing brick, which might be made a very remunerative business; located between the New York and Connecticut markets; steamboat communication with each, and can always obtain the highest price for every variety of produce.

50 acres,	No. 4258,	$800

IN ASHFORD, 2 miles from Westford Glass Factory and 6 from Stafford Springs depot; 10 acres of heavy wood; 1 story house, 26 × 30, L, 12 × 16; 1 barn, etc.; good well with pump; offered low.

80 Acres,	No. 4259,	$2,400

IN SOUTH COVENTRY; 1½ story house 30 x 40, with a wing; just put in excellent order; barn, wagon, corn, and wood house, etc.; ten acres to wood, short distance from the H. P. & F. R. R.; fine orchard in full bearing adjoins the garden; pleasant and desirable location for a country residence, a short distance from a public school and three churches; stock and tools if wanted.

60 Acres,	No. 4259,	$2,600

IN SOUTH COVENTRY, one mile from Center, near by school, etc.; twenty-six acres of mowing and tillage; choice fruit; land smooth, and under good cultivation; keeps ten head of cattle, two horses, and a flock of sheep; one story and L house, painted white; good barn and shed, carriage and tool house, hog house, etc.; $1,300 cash.

20 Acres,	No. 4260,	$3,600

IN ELLINGTON, on Main street; a beautiful village residence, with twenty acres of extra nice land, free from stone; abundance of select fruit trees and vines; nice dwelling, containing ten rooms; aqueduct water in the house from spring; good barn, etc.; $1,800 cash.

12 Acres,	No. 4261,	$12,000

IN HARTFORD, just outside of city limits; 12¼ acres, all A No. 1 land, and newly fenced; nice brick two story house, with L, painted drab; nice new barn, carriage shed, tool and work shop; considerable fruit; water in the house, water-closet, etc.

130 Acres,	No. 4262,	$2,500

IN HARTLAND, 1½ miles from Center; about twenty acres to wood, balance tillage, mowing, and pasture; well watered and fenced; has some fruit; 1½ story house, barn, two cow houses, tobacco shed, etc.

30 Acres,   No. 4263, $3,800

In North Glastenbury, four miles from Hartford; all good land; young fruit, not in bearing; two story house, painted white, good barn; good well at house and barn; one-fourth mile from school, one mile from church, near stores, etc.; located on main road.

50 Acres,   No. 4264, $4,000

In Avon, one mile from Collinsville depot; fifteen to twenty acres of wood; seventeen varieties of apples, fifteen of pears, four of grapes, five of cherries, strawberries, cranberries, currants, etc.; land is well watered and fenced, and under good cultivation; large two story and L house, in good order, barn, carriage house, cow shed, etc.; near school, church, and good neighbors; will exchange for a smaller farm.

175 Acres,   No. 4265, $8,000

In Durham, three miles west of Connecticut river, 1½ from Durham Center; wood enough to pay for it; two dwelling houses, nearly new, each two story with L, painted and blinded; three large barns, horse barn, shed, etc ; aqueduct water to buildings; a large variety of fruit; picket fences, shrubbery, etc.; $4,000 cash.

Grist mill, etc.,   No. 4266, $10,000

One of the best mills in the State; 2½ story, 36 × 50, painted and sanded; five run four foot stone: four for flour and feed, one for plaster; three bolts, one scourer, one overshot and one breast wheel, stone dam, etc.; grater cider mill, two presses, hay scales, horse shed, dwelling house, 1½ story with L, painted and blinded, barn 24 × 60 feet, hog house, etc.; eleven acres of extra choice land; plenty of apples, cherries, etc.; water power never fails; located one-half mile from center of a thriving village; *sold 300 tons of feed and 300 tons of plaster the last year;* TERMS EASY; *mill alone cost over $11,000, is all in perfect order, etc.*

100 Acres,   No. 4267, $5,500

In Vernon, one mile from Rockville, one-half mile from railroad station; a very desirable farm, well divided, and every lot well watered, and never fails; extra fencing, all got out; *enough to last fifty years;* plenty of wood and timber; keeps eighteen head of stock; two good fruit orchards in bearing; excellent mowing, grass all cut by machine; nice two story and L house, painted and blinded, two barns, tobacco barn, carriage house, two sheds, and wood house; pleasantly located; stock and tools for sale; $2,800 cash.

70 Acres,   No. 4268, $1,300

In Hebron, one mile from Hebron Green, near school, etc.; land is well divided, watered, and fenced; dwelling house, wagon house, new barn 28 x 42, etc.; 175 Concord and Delaware grape vines, thirty-five young apple trees of choice grafted fruit, forty trees of common varieties, eleven peach trees, etc.; offered very low; $1,000 cash.

| 50 Acres, | No. 4269, | $1,800 |

In SOUTH COVENTRY, one mile from Center; pleasantly located, near school and pleasant neighbors; excellent land, and well divided; two story and L house, barn, carriage house, etc.; fruit orchard, and plenty of wood for farm use.

| 55 Acres, | No. 4270, | $650 |

In WEST GRANVILLE, five miles from Riverton, two miles from West Hartland; land suitably divided into mowing, pasture, and wood-land; good dwelling house and barn; some orcharding; 100 sugar maples, timber and wood, etc.; *terms to suit the purchaser.*

| 1 Acre, | No. 4240, | $600 |

In TOLLAND, three-fourths mile from Center, near school, and four miles from Rockville: land is under a high state of cultivation; nice young fruit orchard; row of shade trees in front; house 22 x 28, with L, 18 x 30 wood house attached; barn 18 x 20; $450 cash.

| 140 Acres, | No. 4271, | $6,500 |

In LITCHFIELD, 2½ miles from Center; twelve acres to wood; *will cut* 1,000 *cords*, worth from $5 to $7 in market; balance suitably divided; is a capital dairy farm; well watered and fenced; mowing all done by machine; will keep twenty cows, a pair of horses, and other stock; 100 fruit trees; good two story and L house, with tin roof, painted white and blinded, carriage house, painted, three barns, two sheds, etc., all in good order, and well located; sugar-maple orchard of 100 trees; $3,000 cash; stock and tools may be had.

| Hotel property, | No. 4272, | $28,000 |

In HARTFORD, on MAIN STREET; a valuable hotel property, with livery and sale stables, etc.; new brick barn 92 x 42, with cellar; lot 58 feet front, 100 feet wide in rear, and 220 feet deep; this offers a splendid chance for a *profitable investment.*

| 45 Acres, | No. 4273, | $1,500 |

In EAST GLASTENBURY, one half mile from school and two churches, one-half mile from woolen factory, and nine from Hartford; two story and L house, wants some repairs; good large barn and other outbuildings; wood, fruit, plow, pasture, and mowing land; $1,000 cash.

Blacksmith shop,   No. 4274, $225

In ROCKY HILL; good shop, tools, etc., with interest and good will in the business.

130 Acres,   No. 4275, $2,250

In EASTFORD, five miles from Chaplin; keeps twenty head of cattle the year around; house 24 × 32, in good repair; barn 30 × 60, horse barn, granary, etc.; aqueduct water; 150 sugar-maples, and wood sufficient for the farm; farm is bounded west by Natchaug river; the meadows contain about thirty acres of rich alluvial soil, acknowledged to be the best in town; about one-half of which can be plowed; *cuts no poor hay;* a good dairy or sheep farm.

Large shop, &c.,   No. 4276, $1,500

In FARMINGTON; the large brick building known as the "Phœnix Works," two story, basement and attic; size 35 × 40, with addition 14 × 35: sixty foot stack for steam boiler; the walls are massive, and heavily timbered; suitable for any business; $500 cash.

6 Acres,   No. 4277, $2,000

In CLINTON; good dwelling house and barn; land partly to wood, balance tillage, etc.; *offered low.*

46 Acres, mills, &c.,   No. 4278, $3,000

In NORTH COVENTRY; spool shop, two story, 28 × 42; thirteen feet breast wheel, ten feet buckets; joiners' shop, 34 × 18, 2½ story; patent iron wheel, planing mill, mortise machine, three circular saws, etc.; saw mill, 60 × 18, with a cast iron wheel; shingle mill, 44 × 16, tub wheel, nine feet, etc.; forty-six acres of the best land in the vicinity; house 30 × 40, with L, 16 × 25; wood house 20 × 15, barn 25 × 35, with shed 25 × 16; these mills are situated on a never failing stream, and as the property *must be sold soon we are willing to sacrifice.*

20 Acres, store, &c.,   .   No. 4279, $9,000

In LYME; extra choice land; corner property; one-half mile from steamboat and railway station; excellent house, barn, and outbuildings; also a STORE doing a good trade; will sell the whole, or a part.

Village Residence,   No. 4280, $2,000

In CROMWELL, near three churches, stores, post office, school, &c.; two story and basement house, of twelve rooms; good barn, excellent garden, seven varieties of grapes; pleasantly located, 1¾ miles from Middletown.

200 acres,   No. 4281, $35. to $50. per acre.

In HARWINTON, three miles from center, 1½ story house, with L, tenant house; four barns; sheds; ice house; &c.; 40 acres of meadow, can all be mowed with machine; 40 acres to wood; *estimated to cut 2000 cords, worth $6. per cord in Plymouth*, 4½ *miles distant*, 10 acres of grafted fruit, 100 pear trees, ½ in bearing; one acre of grape vines, about 20 varieties; will sell a part, or the whole.

25 acres,   No. 4282, $1,700

In ANDOVER, 1½ miles from depot, 2 churches, stores, post office, hotel, grist and saw mills, etc.; ⅓ mile from school, and shops; ½ story house 22 × 32, blinded, barn 24 × 30: wood house 18 × 30, with set kettle, etc.; fruit in variety; 11 acres of thrifty woodland, within 50 rods of the house; *offered low.*

1½ acres,   No. 4283, $500

BOLTON, ¼ mile from railroad depot, school, etc.; a one story house, with wood shed, and barn, in fair order, some fruit.

65 acres, distillery, &c., No. 4285, $2,000

In GRANBY, 5 acres to wood, 30 acres mowing and tillage, balance pasture, well watered and fenced, dwelling house, 1½ story, 2 barns, 2 sheds, each 40 feet long; cider mill house, 30 × 40 with fixtures, all new; also one still house, and still, which holds 4½ bbls: good wells, and spring near the house; terms easy.

Mill property,   No. 4286, $1,800

In ANDOVER, water power nine feet head, with privilege of raising dam five feet, shop 25 × 30; 1½ story, with basement 9½ feet between joists, which contains the lathes, heavy saws, and planer; floor above, has three saw frames, three turning lathes, one drill lathe, one scroll saw, frames, etc.; all plentifully furnished, with the necessary implements for carrying on the TOY CABINET WARE MANUFACTURE, which is now in successful operation, third floor has a varnish room, store room, etc.; with benches, presses and all necessary tools; also, if wanted, one dwelling house, barn, and about 35 acres of land, at a moderate price; will sell the property with, or without the machinery and tools.

65 acres,   No. 4287, $2,600

In EAST HADDAM, 1½ miles from Goodspeed's Landing, on Connecticut river, land is suitably divided; timber and wood valued at $2,000; orcharding of choice fruits, dwelling house in good order, painted and blinded, barn 25 × 35, carriage, wood house, etc.: pleasantly located, ⅛ mile from school and church, on main road from Middletown to Lyme, *very cheap.*

8 acres,   No. 4288, $9,000

In HARTFORD, just outside of city limits, a desirable country residence for any gentleman wishing to do business in the city; two story and L house barn, sheds, etc.; variety of fruit and vines.

150 acres,   No. 4289, $1,600

In UNION, two miles from center; divided into woodland, mowing, tillage and pasture; with plenty of fruit; good and convenient buildings, within ½ mile of school; has *wood and timber enough to pay for the farm.*

60 acres,   No. 4290, $3,700

In TOLLAND, one mile from center, ¾ mile from school, etc.; land all good, well fenced with stone, and suitably divided, with water in all the lots; variety of fruits; ten acres of chestnut wood; 1½ story house with L, in good style, painted white and blinded; barn 30 × 36, in good order.

45 acres,   No. 4291, $1,800

In NEW HARTFORD, ¼ mile from school and church; 15 acres to wood, balance mowing and tillage; 120 young fruit trees; ½ story and L, house, good barn and tobacco shed; all in good repair; will exchange for other property.

100 acres,   No. 4292, $2,000

In ASHFORD, one mile from center, ¼ mile from school, etc.; pleasant location, land slopes to the south; 15 acres to wood; fruit, cranberry bog, etc.; two dwelling houses, wood house, carriage house, barn and granary, 200 feet new picket fence, painted; building in good repair.

62 acres,   No. 4293, $10,000

In NEW BRITAIN, one mile from center; 45 acres mowing and tillage, balance pasturage; watered by springs and streams; two young and thrifty apple orchards, in bearing: cherries, pears, vines, etc.; two story house, painted white, barn, horse barn, tobacco shed, cow shed, etc.; all in good order, and pleasantly located; $5,000 cash. Stock and tools may be had.

250 acres,   No. 3159, $10,000

In NEW HARTFORD, about equidistant from Winsted, Collinsville, Wolcottville, and New Hartford; large orchard of choice fruit; capital dairy or stock farm, will keep 30 cows; large amount of wood and timber; *enough to more than pay for it*; two story house; four barns, &c., &c.; will exchange in part for city property.

150 acres,   No. 3154, $2,000

In MARLBORO, near Glastenbury line, 14 miles from Hartford; 50 acres to wood; fruit in variety; keeps 15 to 20 head of stock, sheep, etc.; good house, two barns, one new, with basement; $1,000 cash.

180 acres,   No. 3149, $4,500

In HAMPTON, one mile from center, land under good cultivation, well fenced and watered and suitably divided, has a fine timber lot, only ½ mile from saw mill; cuts forty tons hay, being located near the new Boston and E. R. R., the timber and wood can be sold readily on the ground; two dwellings, three barns, granary, carriage and wood house, etc.

138 acres,   No. 3142, $2,700

In CHAPLIN, 2⅓ miles from centre; 45 acres to wood and timber, balance mowing, tillage, and pasturage; good house and barn, pleasantly located; terms easy.

Mills, &c.,   No. 3141, $4,500

In CHAPLIN, two miles from centre; grist mill, saw mill, machine shop, trip hammer shop, blacksmith shop, two dwelling houses, barn, etc.; mills all supplied with necessary machinery, and doing a good business, three acres of land with the houses, etc.; terms easy.

30 acres,   No. 3196, $5,000

In SOUTH WINDSOR, 1¼ miles from Buckland station; land is under high cultivation; 60 choice fruit trees, etc.; has one good dwelling house and one old one; barn, tobacco house, carriage house and horse barn; shed, etc.; aqueduct water in house and barn; only 8 miles from Hartford.

100 acres,   No. 3187, $12,000

In EAST GRANBY, ½ mile from Center; 10 acres to wood, balance choice tillage and mowing; abundance of fruits; keeps about 25 head of stock; 2 story and L house, painted and blinded; barn, wood and carriage house, horse barn, granary, tobacco barn, sheds, etc.; aqueduct water from spring to house and barn.

47 acres,   No. 3186, $3,000

In BERLIN, ½ mile from railroad station and 2½ from Berlin Center; land is good and early; somewhat uneven, but not stony; 225 young fruit trees partially in bearing; old style house, in fair order; barn with basement; a fine, never failing stream waters the meadows and pastures.

50 acres,   No. 3183, $1,000

In WINDHAM; has wood and timber enough to pay for it; near school, etc.; good 1½ story house, carriage house and large barn.

50 acres,   No. 3182, $1,800

In MANCHESTER, 2½ miles from Cheneyville; good house and barn; some wood and fruit; land is very good; raises excellent tobacco, etc.

174 acres,   No. 3169, $2,000

In CHAPLIN, 5½ miles from Willimantic; will keep well 15 head of cattle, etc.; 1½ story house with L, newly covered and painted; new barn, 26 x 50; shed 40 feet long; considerable wood, etc.; stock and tools for sale.

110 acres,   No. 3130, $2,800

In CHAPLIN, ½ mile from Centre, 5 miles from Willimantic, and about 2 from proposed depot of the Boston, Hartford and Erie Railroad; 30 acres to timber and wood; abundance of select fruit; land under good cultivation, well watered and fenced; keeps through the year 15 head of cattle, flock of sheep, horse, etc.; good house with L; 2 large barns, both with fine basements; store house, etc.

200 acres,   No. 3125, $7,000

In SCOTLAND; pleasantly located, about 6 miles from Willimantic; one of the best stock farms in Windham county; nice 2 story and L house; painted and blinded; tenant house, 3 barns, sheds, etc., etc. will keep 50 head of stock throughout the year; also, may be had, 80 acres, detached, for $800, comprising wood and pasture land; terms easy.

Shops, &c.,   No. 3116, $4,000

In CROMWELL, 1½ miles from steamboat wharf on Connecticut river, and 3 from city of Middletown; 2 story shop, 26 x 35, with wings, 24 x 36; 18 ft. wheel; fine water power, never fails; 2 story house, etc., with 6 acres of land.

70 acres,   No. 3067, $2,000

In CHAPLIN, ½ mile from the Center; a finely located farm; land under good cultivation; lies on east bank of Natchaug river; good 1½ story house with L; carriage and wood house, milk house, barn with aqueduct water in yard; shed, with hay-loft; tenant house; choice fruit, etc.; must be sold to close an estate.

300 acres,   No. 3059, $7,000

In NEW HARTFORD; 70 acres timberland; one of the best dairy and stock farms in the county; abundance of fruit, etc.; 2 nice dwellings, 5 barns, 4 cow houses, horse barn, ice house, etc.; will exchange for city or other good property.

75 acres,   L, No. 171, $1,500

In WESTFORD, 2 miles from the village; land suitably divided into mowing and tillage, pasture and woodland; 150 young apple trees, just beginning to bear; pear trees, peaches, cherries, etc.; 12 head of stock on the farm for sale if wanted.

34 acres,   L, No. 172, $2,300

In FARMINGTON, 2 miles from Center and 7 from Hartford; excellent land; variety of apples, pears, cherries, plums, grapes, etc.; $\frac{1}{4}$ mile from school, and but 4 miles from New Britain; very pleasantly located and offered low; $1\frac{1}{2}$ story house, painted white; barn, tobacco house, woodshed, etc.

55 acres,   L, No. 174, $12,500

In WEST HARTFORD, $3\frac{1}{2}$ miles from Hartford; land is very choice, and suitable for any New England crop; 3 nice apple orchards; pears, grapes, etc.; nice large dwelling house, painted and blinded; large barn and other out buildings; terms $4,500 cash.

12 acres,   L, No. 175, $1,400

In BLOOMFIELD, only 6 miles from Hartford; land is good and well cultivated; young fruit trees of apple, peach, cherry, etc., in bearing; new $1\frac{1}{2}$ story house, painted white and blinded; new barn, etc.; may be had with stock, tools, etc., for $2,000.

Timber lot, 27 acres,   R, No. 3, $1,000

In UNION, 5 miles from Stafford Springs depot; comprised mostly of chestnut and oak timber; offered far below its value.

51 acres,   R, No. 5, $2,500

In SOMERS, $\frac{3}{4}$ mile from Somersville, near Shaker Village; land is excellent and suitably divided; watered by a never failing stream; good cranberry marsh; has a small 1 story house and barn; buildings are not very good; also, 8 acres on the mountain, ($3\frac{1}{2}$ miles distant,) covered with wood and timber; may be had for $200; terms $\frac{1}{2}$ cash.

| 135 acres, | R, No. 10, | $3,500 |

In TOLLAND, 1½ miles from Tolland street, containing 135 acres well divided into tillage, pasture, mowing and wood-land; good house, 2 large barns, wood house, etc., with 2 wells of water; there are now growing on the premises 1000 Concord grape vines, from which two to three thousand pounds of grapes may be obtained yearly: also, 7 acres cranberries, 1 of strawberries, 50 dwarf apple and pear trees, and a large lot of peach, cherry and plum trees, and grafted apple trees. The fruit will soon pay for the property, which is near good markets; this is a rare chance for a man who wishes to go into the fruit culture, aside from the farming operations; crop, stock and tools for sale.

| Mills, &c., | No. 2187, | $6,000 |

In BURLINGTON, 6 miles from Farmington, 2 from Collinsville, 2½ from Unionville, etc.; shop, 40 × 40; 3 story and attic, machinery, &c.; water power sufficient to drive any machinery, and never fails; R. R. track to the factory; dwelling house, 2 story, with L, barn, &c., all painted; garden comprises one acre land.

| 114 acres, | L, No. 176, | very cheap. |

NEAR BALTIC, in town of Scotland, a short distance from R. R. Stations, Eagleville and Occum Villages, &c.; over 600 cords wood on the farm; house, 1½ story, with L; barn and other buildings. Or, will sell 40 acres with buildings, and ⅓ of the woodland. ALSO, 30 acres woodland, lying near the farm. We offer this property *cheap*, as it was purchased to secure *flowage*, and is not wanted by the present owners.

| 12 acres, | L, No. 177, | $1,100 |

In WEST AVON, twelve acres of land with a good, comfortable old style house, barn, &c.

| 3¾ acres, | No. 1119, | $12,000 |

In HARTFORD, just outside of city limits, on one of the best streets in the suburbs; a fine large brick residence with modern improvements; stables, sheds, &c. The land is extra choice for early gardening and fruits, and is altogether one of the most desirable places at the price offered, to be found around Hartford.

| 55 acres, | L. No. 179, | $3,200 |

In SOUTHINGTON. A GOOD CHANCE FOR SOMEBODY. A farm of 55 acres with house, barn and all necessary out-buildings, pleasantly situated 1¼ mile from R. R. Station; about half way between Hartford and New Haven; has a nice house containing 10 or 11 rooms, with fine cellar, wood-shed, &c.; good well; nice apple orchard, grapes, currants, quinces, strawberries, &c.; buildings are all in good condition: the land consists of 20 acres valuable woodland, 35 acres in meadow, pasture, plowing, &c.; some 5 or 6 acres are to clover and rye; will sell stock, wagon, harness, hay and grain, and farm implements, &c.; the whole for only $3,500; terms easy.

| Fruit Farm, | L. 189, | For sale low. |

AT SOUTH PASS, SOUTHERN ILLINOIS.

| 30 acres, | R. No. 15, | $2,800 |

IN ENFIELD, 1 mile from Hazardville, 3 from Thompsonville, and about 8 from Springfield; 7 acres to wood, balance all tillage and mowing; level and free from stone; Excellent house 2 story L, nice barn and shed; buildings all pa'nted and in first class order; location one of the pleasantest in the country; has the finest row of maples in front of the premises to be found in the state. *This farm has never been offered before for less than $3,500, and is very cheap at that sum; we now offer it less than value of buildings;* satisfactory reasons for selling.

| 130 acres, | R. No. 14, | $5,300 |

IN VERNON, only 1½ mile from Rockville and Vernon depots; 7 acres to wood; balance to excellent mowing, tillage and pasturage; land smooth, uses machines; 1 1-2 story house with 2 Ls, (convenient for two families,) painted white and blinded, and pleasantly located; barn 32 x 40; horse barn and wagon shed; tobacco house 18 x 36; granary, &c. $2000 may remain on mortgage. *A desirable farm and cheap.*

| Mills, &c. | L. No. 183, | $2,800 |

IN WINTHROP, town of Saybrook, a valuable manufacturing privilege with a large mill; has 3000 square feet of floor; 2 dams, new wheel, machinery, &c. &c.; now doing a large business; terms, $1,800 cash.

| 100 acres, | No. L. 176, | $5,000 |

IN EAST HADDAM, 2¼ miles from three steamboat landings on Connecticut river, in a pleasant and desirable location, among first class society, 100 acres excellent land suitably divided; two dwelling houses, barns, etc.; excellent fruit in bearing, could be divided into two good farms of 50 acres each, stock and tools for sale.

| 12 acres, $7,000 | No. R. 11, | 5 acres, $5,000 |

FRUIT FARM IN WEST HARTFORD, a place of twelve acres, situated on the main street, one mile south of the center. The fruit consists of about one hundred apple trees of the best kinds, all young and just come into bearing; two hundred grape vines, set out last spring, principally Iona, Allen's, Hybrid, and Delaware. Also, pear trees, strawberries, raspberries.

and other fruits. The property is divided by the highway, five acres being
on the east side and seven on the west, giving a street front of about seven
hundred and fifty feet. The buildings, are house, barn, and green house,
all in good repair, will sell with or without stock and crops, will sell 5 acres
and buildings for $5,000.

| 18 acres, | No. R. 18, | $2,600 |

In LEBANON, ON LIBERTY HILL, near by church, store, post office,
school, etc.; 18 acres choice land, fine apple orchard of 2 acres select fruit
in full bearing, pears, cherries, quinces, etc., excellent buildings all in
order; nice 2 story and L. house, painted white and blinded; good large
barn, carriage, and wood house, granary, etc.; is known as "*the Commodore
Champlin Place.*" *The house alone is worth $3,000*; a portion of the land
is *cheap at $100 per acre; we offer in this a rare bargain.*

| 80 acres, | No. R. 16, | $3,500 |

NEAR MANSFIELD DEPOT, excellent farm, producing large crops, well
fenced, and watered, suitably divided, etc.; nearly new, 2 story and L,
house painted white, a very superior barn, with basement, shed, granary,
etc.; *the buildings cannot be replaced for $6,000.*

| 68 acres, | R. 21, | $6,250 |

In LEBANON, 1¾ mile from station on N. L. R. R., near by school, 1 mile
from the village church, post office, grist mill, shop, etc.; land is choice,
about 5 acres oak and hickory wood; mowing done by machine, land well
watered, choice fruit, etc.; nice modern style 2 story and L house, painted
white and blinded; 11 rooms, bath room, etc.; stock, barn 24 × 60, with
24 feet shed; horse barn, 22 × 32, with shed, etc.; all in order, and pleasantly located, only 10 miles from Norwich; farm keeps 15 head of stock
year round, will keep more; *must be sold, and is offered exceedingly low.*

| ¼ acre, | R. 22, | $3,600 |

In NEW BRITAIN VILLAGE, on Park Street, a nice new double house,
one tenement on each side of about 7 rooms each, house 2 story and L,
painted white and blinded; cemented cellar, concrete walks in front, to,
and around the house; lot 6½ rods front × 8 rods deep, enclosed by picket
fence painted white; *will rent and pay over 10 per cent.* This desirable
property is offered *low*, or, *will exchange for a farm worth $3,000, or $4,000.*

| Village Residence, &c., | L, 188, | $1,500 |

In MANSFIELD, a nice 2 story and L house, painted white, etc.; with a
barn and a few acres land; *will exchange for a farm worth $1,500 or $2,500.*

61 acres,   L, 187,   cheap.

IN LONGMEADOW, MASS., *an unusual opportunity to buy* a first class farm at a low price, pleasantly located on the main road, five miles South of Springfield, and two and a half North of Thompsonville, Ct., in an excellent neighborhood, near schools and convenient to church, post office and depot.

The farm is easy to till, and will produce any crop grown in the valley of the Connecticut, including tobacco. It is well fenced and conveniently divided into mowing—including a splendid eleven acre lot of river bottom land—tillage, pasturage and wood land. It has an orchard of over one hundred trees, besides a large variety of small fruits. Running water in the pasture and meadow and a never-failing supply at the house and barn.

The house is two stories, with L, painted white, green blinds, ten rooms in main part, besides halls and closets, all in FIRST CLASS order and condition. Barn sixty feet long, corn-barn, pig-house, tool-house, etc.; fine shade and ornamental trees.

A PARTIAL LIST

OF

CITY PROPERTY

FOR SALE BY

C. A. LINCOLN,

Real Estate Broker,

NO. 265 MAIN STREET,

HARTFORD, CONN.

ON ANN STREET. House and lot, $11,000.

ON ANN STREET. Double house and lot, $6,200.

ON ELLERY STREET. Two houses, $1,300 and $2,000.

ON MAIN STREET. Brick house and lot, $6,000.

ON CHESTNUT STREET. House and lot, $7,000.

ON WINDSOR AVENUE. House, barn, and five acres, $6,000.

ON GRAND STREET. Two houses and lots, $3,500.

ON BLUE HILLS. House, barn, and 12¼ acres, $12,000.

ON CENTRE STREET. Two double houses, $7,000, each.

ON BELLEVUE STREET. A double house and lot cheap.

ON WOLCOTT STREET. A double house and lot, $3,500.

ON WASHINGTON STREET. A fine residence and lot, $13,000.

ON CANTON STREET. Two houses and lots, $5,000, each.

ON AFFLECK STREET. Three houses and lots, $5,000 to $8,000.

ON MORGAN STREET. House and lot, $6,500.

ON HUDSON STREET. Six houses and lots, $4,500 to $7,000.

4

ON BUCKINGHAM STREET. House and lot, 11,000.

ON ASYLUM AVENUE. House and lot, $11,000.

ON ASYLUM AVENUE. House and lot, $12,000.

FOR SALE ON STATE STREET. A valuable block.

ON FARMINGTON AVENUE. Residence and lot, $15,000.

ON GOVERNOR STREET. A good property for investment.

ON DEAN STREET. House and lot, $2,200.

ON GOVERNOR STREET. House, barn and lot, cheap.

ON VINE STREET. House, barn, and eight acres, $9,000.

ON VINE STREET. House, barn, and eight acres, $6,500.

ON FARMINGTON AVENUE. Several elegant residences, with from one to fifty acres of land, at prices from $15,000 to $50,000.

ON HUDSON STREET. A large double house, with two very convenient tenements in either half; large lot, &c.; the whole for less than $6,000.

ON HUDSON STREET. Two single brick houses for $4,500 and $5,500 : each contains two good tenements, with good lots, fruit, vines, &c.

ON ZION STREET. A two story and L house, containing three tenements; lot 75 × 320; the rear fronting on Putnam street 75 feet—a good bargain.

ON HUDSON STREET. Single brick house, and lot suitable for two families, for $4,500. Also one for $5,500.

ON VINE STREET. Brick house, barn, sheds, &c., with 8 acres choice land for early market gardening, well stocked with fruits, &c.

ON CANTON STREET. Two brick houses—two tenements in each—both in perfect order, and good investments. Price $5,000 each.

ON CHESTNUT STREET. A single brick house, brick barn, and good lot cheap. Also, a single frame house, very desirable, and furnished with gas and water, furnace, range, &c. Good lot, with fruit and vines.

ON WALNUT STREET. A first class double house, each half contains all the modern improvements, nearly new and in perfect order. Will sell either half, or the whole at a bargain.

ON WETHERSFIELD AVENUE. A brick house, two nice tenements, very large lot, everything in good order. Price $5,000.

ON BLUE HILLS. A very desirable residence, with stables and outbuildings, and 12 acres of choice land, fruits, vines, &c., for $12,000.

ON GROVE STREET. Brick house and large lot, stocked with fruit trees, &c. House contains most of the modern improvements and is very centrally located—only a few steps from the post-office, price about $7,000.

ON CHESTNUT STREET. A nice single house of 12 rooms, large lot, fruit trees, vines, &c., $7,000.

Double brick house of four tenements on Center street—a good investment, $7,000.

ON COLLEGE STREET, near Main Street, a fine large building lot, at a low price for cash, or in exchange for improved city property.

A very desirable single residence, with fine lot, choice fruits in variety, &c.; house contains about twelve rooms, furnished with gas and water, furnace, range, bath room, closets, &c.; located in the south part of the city, a few rods west of Main street.

An elegant residence and grounds in the south part of the city; altogether one of the finest residences in town; replete with every modern convenience, and is offered at a very reasonable price—on terms to suit the purchaser; a fine brick stable and a large amount of land can be purchased with it if desired.

A SNUG SINGLE HOUSE on Whitman court, between Buckingham and College streets, near Main street, very low and terms unusually easy.

ON FARMINGTON AVENUE. A nice residence, barn and eight acres very choice land; great abundance of select fruit, &c., for about $10,000.

ON CHARTER OAK PLACE. The finest building lot in Hartford.

FOR SALE. A brick block on Commerce street, suitable for heavy manufacturing purposes; 2d story, size 45 × 70 feet; lot 70 × 100 feet.

ON TEMPLE STREET. A good single brick house and lot—would be a good business property. Price $3,500.

ON CHAPEL STREET. A snug brick house with good lot suitable for barn and drive-way; very pleasantly and centrally situated, near Trumbull and only a few steps from Main street. A bargain at $6,700.

ON FARMINGTON AVENUE. A first class residence and fine lot—a corner property. We call it cheap at $15,000.

ON WALNUT STREET. Between R. R. and High street, a very pleasant double brick house, all in perfect order, with good lot, &c. The whole for $13,000. Terms, $4,000 cash—balance can remain on mortgage.

ON BELLEVUE STREET. A very nice large single brick house of two genteel tenements, gas, water, marbles, &c., with brick barn and large lot. Also, a double house of two tenements each.

ON WADSWORTH STREET. A very desirable single brick house, modern conveniences, large lot, choice fruit, etc; price $8,000. Also, a single brick house for $5,500. Also, a single brick house and good lot for $7,000.

FOR SALE ON CEDAR STREET. Must be closed out soon. Single brick house, two tenements, &c. Price only $2,500. Terms very easy.

ON SQUIRES STREET. A single brick residence and large lot; worth $8,000. Also, half of double brick house, two nice tenements, gas and water; price $2,700—very cheap. Also, a single house for only $2,300.

The snug single house and lot No. 8 Green street, for only $2,500. Terms easy.

ON WINDSOR STREET. South of Pleasant street, a brick house of 15 rooms, gas, water, etc. Price $3,300.

ON MAIN STREET. Several first class residences, worth from $18,000 to $30,000.

ON LAFAYETTE STREET. A large single brick residence with a very large lot, choice fruit trees, vines, etc. Price only $8,500.

A CAPITAL INVESTMENT. A nice new block of fourteen tenements; rents to a good class of tenants; pays about thirteen per cent on the price asked.

ON RUSSELL STREET. A brick house, east half of double house, has a good lot stocked with fruit trees, vines, etc. Price $2,500.

ON WASHINGTON STREET. A first class residence and lot. House nearly new and replete with all the modern improvements. Price *very low*—only $13,000. Will be sold furnished if wanted, and give possession any time. Terms easy.

ON SHELDON STREET. A nice, large residence, and a large lot of land, suitable for building lots. Good property for an investment.

ON MAIN STREET. Several desirable pieces of property worth from $15,000 to $60,000. Desirable as investments.

ON WINTHROP STREET. A first class house and large lot, stocked with fruit trees, vines, &c., for $15,000.

ON BENTON STREET. Brick house near the depot of the Hartford and Wethersfield Horse Railway Co.; two tenements, &c. Price only $4,000. Terms to suit.

ON PARK STREET. A single brick house of good size with large lot, shrubbery, vines, etc. Price $3,500.

SPLENDID BUILDING SITE and land for sale—beautifully located just outside of city limits, and commands one of the *most extensive and grandest views* in New England. The property consists of 20 acres choice land; has 500 feet front on two streets; has a nice barn with basement; good well of water at the barn, and land well watered; has 65 choice, thrifty fruit trees in full bearing. Price very low for so desirable a property.

ON WETHERSFIELD AVENUE, almost within the city limits, three acres of choice land, stocked with select fruit, and is by far the best building site on the avenue. This property has not been offered for sale before, but can now be had at a great bargain. Terms, only $2,000, cash.

DESIRABLE LOT on Farmington avenue, size, 150 by 250. For sale at a bargain. Terms easy.

ON ANN STREET—a first class residence, replete with all the modern improvements, containing 17 very pleasant and conveniently arranged rooms, good lot, choice fruit, vines, &c. We offer this residence at a very low price, as we desire to dispose of it immediately. Terms made easy.

ON PROSPECT HILL—a choice place of five acres, land well adapted for *early market gardening*, &c. Only half a mile from the city limits; plenty of fruit, vines, &c.

A NICE DOUBLE BRICK HOUSE, barn and large lot on Affleck street; contains four tenements of six rooms each; water and gas on every floor. This property will pay well to rent; would make a very desirable boarding house of twenty-four rooms, being very handy to the shops of Pratt, Whitney & Co., Sharps' Rifle Co., &c. Will exchange.

A FINE BRICK RESIDENCE of two tenements, furnished with marble mantles, grates, cemented cellar, gas, water, etc., with a fine large lot, well stocked with vines, shrubs, etc., and on one of the pleasantest and most desirable streets in the north part of the city, only a few rods from street cars, etc. Price only $6,500. Terms easy.

FOR SALE—On Buckingham street, a first-class residence, nearly new, and one of the most desirable houses on the street; furnished with all the modern improvements, and finished throughout in a very superior manner. We offer this property for $11,000, as the owner is about to leave the state and desires to sell immediately.

FIRST CLASS RESIDENCES in all parts of the city. No prudent buyer will purchase before examining my extensive list, which includes some of the finest residences in Hartford, at all prices, from $10,000 to $50,000, and any number of houses and lots from $1,500 to $10,000.

FOR A GOOD AND SAFE INVESTMENT, I offer several fine double brick Residences; for first-class tenants that pay from 12 to 16 per cent. on the price.

ON GRAND STREET. A nice single brick residence of two tenements; a good garden and yard, &c. Price $4,000. Terms unusually easy. Do not rent a house when you can buy such property as this on the easy terms we offer it at.

Splendid First-Class Residence,

On one of the best streets in Hartford. New house, new furniture, carpets, beds and bedding, even "the baby's crib," and a thousand and one articles; winter's stock of coal; and everything wanted in housekeeping. The whole for less than $15,000 !—not the value of house alone.

ELEGANT RESIDENCES AND GROUNDS, on Washington, Main, Ann, Buckingham, Charter Oak Place, Asylum and Farmington Avenues, at all prices, from $18,000 to $40,000.

MAIN AND ASYLUM ST. PROPERTY. Several first-class investments on these and other streets, worthy the inspection of capitalists.

MAIN ST. One of the most desirable places in the city or vicinity. Large lot, handsomely graded and laid out in good taste; shrubbery and fruit trees of choice kinds, comprising apples, peaches, cherries, plums, pears, quinces; red, black and white raspberries; blackberries, strawberries, currants, grapes, &c., &c. Good barn and carriage house; house pleasant, roomy and convenient throughout, and all the buildings in proper repair; located near horse railroad, and offers a rare chance to secure a pleasant home at a bargain. Will not be long in the market. Price $12,000.

ON AVON ST. A large, single brick house, suitable for two families, 8 or 9 rooms each; gas, water, range, &c., in each tenement. Brick barn, and very large lot stocked with fruits. Price $10,500.

ON CHARTER OAK PLACE. One of the most elegant and desirable residences in the city. We offer it low, as the owner is about to leave the state. Price $26,000.

ON MORGAN ST. A large single brick residence, with good lot and very desirably located, near Main st. Barn, &c. Price $

ON MORRIS ST. A nice single brick house, a few steps from Wethersfield avenue, horse railroad, &c. Only $6,600—cheap.

GRIST MILLS AND MANUFACTORIES. I offer for sale five or six good grist mills, located in different parts of the State.

ONE OF THE OLDEST and best established STOVE and TIN WARE STORES in Hartford, doing a large and lucrative business. Stock, tools and good will in the business for sale at a bargain. Also, lease of the store and tenement, or will sell the real estate if wanted. Terms easy.

LEASE, FURNITURE, FIXTURES, and good will, of one of the most central HOTELS in the city of Hartford, doing a good business. For sale cheap—terms easy.

FOR SALE, the Stock, Fixtures, Lease, and good will, of one of the best MARKETS in the city—on Main st. I have a party who will take one-half interest in the above, with some reliable person.

THE KNITTING MILL, at North Manchester Station, near Hartford, having been put in running order, is now offered for sale at a great bargain, consisting of two sets of Cards, and all machinery for manufacturing Woolen or Cotton and Woolen Yarns, with superior Knitting Machines for shirts and drawers, or hosiery. There are also two nice residences, one or both can go with it if wished. It is more delightfully and conveniently situated both for manufacturing and for a residence, than is often found.

HOTEL PROPERTY AND LIVERY STABLES, in one of the most thriving villages on the Connecticut river—offered at a bargain—with or without the personal property.

BAKERY FOR SALE—in one of the most enterprising towns in the state, doing a large business. Lease of premises for five years if wanted, at a low rent. Everything in perfect order requisite for carrying on an extensive business. For sale in consequence of inability of owner to carry it on from ill health. We offer a bargain.

FOR SALE. Chance to engage in a profitable business already established, requiring but a very small capital. Any one desirous of engaging in a safe and lucrative business can hear of an excellent opportunity by en_quiring at this office. Satisfactory reasons will be given by the owner for selling out.

VALUABLE HOTEL PROPERTY, on Main st., with Livery Stables, &c., for sale at a bargain, on easy terms.

ONE OF THE BEST WATER PRIVILEGES IN CONNECTICUT, with Grist Mill, Saw Mill, Shingle Mill, two dwellings, barn, &c., with a farm of 20 acres, all for less than $5,000. Located on a durable stream: never fails; has 42 *Feet Head and Fall.* Mills are in good running order; plenty of custom; has 5 good wheels, etc.; nearly new.

TO RENT—ON MAIN ST. A fine large Store and first-class Residence, for a term of years. The stock, fixtures and good will in the business for sale. A splendid chance to secure a long established and lucrative business. Not to rent unless stock is purchased.

AGENTS WANTED—SOMETHING NEW. Patent Wash Board. One of the best and cheapest Washing Machines in the country. Price only $2.00—within the reach of all; no family should be without it a single washing-day. Chance to coin money. Town, county, state or United States rights for sale or exchange.

ON MAIN STREET—A CIGAR STORE. Stock, Lease, fixtures and good will at a *bargain.*

ON NEW BRITAIN AVENUE—A Grocery Store and Saloon, with tenements over the Store—will sell or rent it *low.*

FRUIT AND CONFECTIONERY STORE, &c., in this city—doing a good business—will sell *at inventory.*

FACTORY PROPERTY FOR SALE.

Valuable Mills and Privileges in Manchester, Cromwell, Chaplin, Mansfield, Scotland, Chatham, &c., &c. Parties wishing to dispose of property of this sort should not fail to give me a call.

MONEY CONSTANTLY ON HAND,

to make advances upon Bond and Mortgage. Also, Mortgages bought and sold.

EXCHANGES OF REAL ESTATE.

City Property to Exchange for Farms.
FARMS TO EXCHANGE FOR CITY PROPERTY.

We are receiving new property for sale every day; having had long experience, and acquired a thorough knowledge of our business, we can give the purchaser advice that will prove beneficial in selecting and purchasing property from our extensive list. Parties wishing to purchase in any locality, will be furnished with full and accurate descriptions of all property we have for sale in the location desired.

DO NOT BUY until you have visited this office, and examined the large list of property of every description, which is left EXCLUSIVELY WITH ME for sale, as you can obtain at this office, FREE, more information in a few moments in regard to property for sale, than you would get in searching the country over the whole season,' ALL SALES OR EXCHANGES at this office, *strictly confidential* when desired.

☞Splendid Suburban Residences, Houses,· Lots, Farms, Manufactories, Mills, Water Privileges, &c.,

of every description, for Sale, Exchange, or to Let.

C. A. LINCOLN, Office 265 MAIN ST.,
HARTFORD, CONN.

NOTICES OF THE PRESS.

"REAL ESTATE.—C. A. Lincoln is one of the oldest real estate brokers doing business in this city, and his operations have been very extensive. His facilities for making purchases or effecting sales can not be surpassed. His office has long been known as the 'Head Center' for New England in all real estate matters. He offers for sale over 500 farms and any amount of other property—and still he says, "I want 300 more farms, &c., as I am selling them off rapidly.' His motto suits the people—' No sale no pay."—*Hartford Post.*

" *Over $53,000 worth of real estate, mostly farms,* was sold by C. A. Lincoln, real estate broker, at his office yesterday. *He actually sold, for Cash, twelve different properties at private sale.* We should consider it a big day's work. If any of our readers have real estate for sale, we advise them to leave their property with him, and we can assure them they will not remain under their own shingles long."—*Hartford Press.*

"REAL ESTATE BROKERS AND REAL ESTATE SALES.—We notice by our exchanges that C. A. Lincoln, Esq., 265 Main street, Hartford, is selling an immense amount of Farm Property and real estate of every description in all sections of the country; and why not? He is an enterprising, wide-awake, clever fellow, has hosts of friends, advertises far and near, and deals liberally with everybody. He is a practical farmer himself, understands his business, and his sales for the past ten years have been enormous, and are constantly increasing. If any of our readers have any real estate for sale, we advise them to employ him to dispose of it, as *he* will dispose of it if anybody can ; besides, his motto is, ' No sale, no pay.' "—*Willimantic Journal.*

" Buyers of real estate for the past few years have been in the habit of going direct to a broker, as they can there obtain (free) more information in five minutes, than they would get in searching the country over a whole season ; and those wanting to sell will ' take due notice thereof, and govern themselves accordingly.' "—*Hartford Times.*

" We called in at the office of C. A. LINCOLN, Real Estate Broker, yesterday, and were surprised to witness the amount of business he is

5

doing in *selling* real estate of every description on commission. His office was *thronged* with buyers and sellers from every part of the country; and we did not wonder that his sales were very large. The fact is, he is a *wide-awake, reliable gentleman to deal with*, and the people like his ways of doing business."—*Hartford Daily Courant.*

"THE WAY TO SELL FARMS.—If any of the farmers in this vicinity wish to sell out we would advise them to put their real estate into the hands of C. A. Lincoln, real estate broker, Hartford, who is one of those active fellows, that is entirely out of his element unless he is buying or selling. If any one wishes ' to buy a farm ' he will suit him short meter. He goes on the principle of ' no sale no pay,' and if any one has not fully made up his mind to sell he had better not employ Mr. Lincoln, for it would go off so quick that there would be no time to back out. The fact is, he is a wide-awake, liberal, and reliable gentleman to deal with ; advertises extensively far and near, and is universally known as one of the most successful dealers in real estate in the whole country, and during the past ten years his sales have been enormous and are constantly increasing. His business has become so extensive that he now publishes a *Conn. Real Estate Register* at an expense of $3000 a year and sends it free to any address all over the United States."—*State Paper.*

CONCLUSION.

THIS closes the first number of THE CONNECTICUT REAL ESTATE REGISTER, which we present gratuitously to the public, with as full and accurate descriptions as is possible, of every variety of property, fresh from the owners. THE REGISTER is now *fully established*, and will be issued semi-annually: from present indications we think the next issue will reach a CIRCULATION OF NEARLY 25,000 COPIES, making it one of the best advertising mediums in the country.

We admit no Advertisements in this issue.

IN OUR NEXT ISSUE, we shall admit a limited number.

EVERY BRANCH OF TRADE should have its representative in these columns, and as *we shall admit none but honest upright dealers*, we shall cheerfully recommend them to our patrons. *From our own office in the usual course of our business, we guarantee it a free circulation of* 6,000 COPIES. The balance of our subscribers we shall obtain *by advertising the Register in every part of the country*, SENT FREE TO ANY ADDRESS POST PAID ON RECEIPT OF TWO STAMPS.

C. A LINCOLN, HARTFORD, CONN.

www.ingramcontent.com/pod-product-compliance
Lightning Source LLC
Chambersburg PA
CBHW031754090426
42739CB00008B/1006